101 of the best
CORPORATE
TEAM-BUILDING
ACTIVITIES

Simon Priest, Ph.D.
& Karl Rohnke

A publication of
TARRAK Technologies

www.tarrak.com
info@tarrak.com

Dedicated to **Michael Gass**

A good friend, humble expert, and highly altruistic professional.

Acknowledgements

Grateful thanks are given to those who continue to share their creativity by offering these activities without thought of renumeration or notoriety. They play the games because they need to; they share the games because they want to.

WAIVER

By choosing to use the events in this book, you recognize that the responsibility for physical and psychological safety rests with you and your clients (not the authors or publishers). You understand that you are free to modify these events in any reasonable manner; however, interpreting or following the directions, safety, planning, and variations contained herein is your responsibility and not ours.

By using these events, you agree NOT to sue any of us! The lawyers would put it this way. *You agree not to hold liable and to fully remise, release, absolve, and forever discharge, waive, save harmless, protect, and keep totally indemnified; Simon Priest, Karl Rohnke, TARRAK Technologies, any book sellers or distributors, and all of their employees or volunteers; free from and against any loss, liability, claim or damage, including without limitation to all legal fees and costs incurred in connection with such action or actions arising or resulting, directly or indirectly, in whole or in part; from the use of these events; even in the case of any accident due to errors, omissions, commissions, ambiguities, or inaccuracies; and especially from negligence or gross negligence.* That should just about do it!

CONTENTS

Simon's Introduction

First of all, 101 sounded like a good number (and we had to stop somewhere)! However, due to ample variations provided with many of the activities, the number of usable team-building tools and tests is probably over twice that. These activities represent the classics that Karl has written about for years and some new ones I've seen in corporate programs around the world. To give credit where credit is due, the origin of each activity is given as best we can recall and each one is also referenced to its original written form according to the following key:

No.	Code	Book (Author)
18	SB	Silver Bullets (Rohnke)
17	CC	Cowstails and Cobras (Rohnke)
8	QS	QuickSilver (Rohnke & Butler)
5	BBA	Bottomless Bag Again (Rohnke)
3	FSIII	Funn Stuff volume III (Rohnke)
3	FSII	Funn Stuff volume II (Rohnke)
2	FSI	Funn Stuff volume I (Rohnke)
2	BB	Bottomless Baggie (Rohnke)
1	BPA	Back Pocket Adventure (Rohnke & Grout)
6	ZG	Zircon Gorilla (Sikes)
5	EM	Executive Marbles (Sikes)
1	UYN	Use Your Noodle (Cavert & Sikes)
5	GWA	Group Work Activities (Sanders)
4	IG	Initiative Games (Simpson)
3	BM	Book of Metaphors (Gass)
2	TT	Teamwork & Teamplay (Cain & Joliff)
16	NEW	New ones (with mixed attribution)
101		Total Activities (the best ones we know)

At this point I'd like to thank Karl Rohnke and Project Adventure for their pioneer work cataloging and keeping the group initiative activities that are a cornerstone to our professional work. If you want to expand your training and development library, I recommend some of these books that are full of more activities:

Rohnke, K. (1984). Silver Bullets. Dubuque, IA: Kendall/Hunt and Project Adventure. (ISBN 0-8403-5682-X).

Rohnke, K. (1989). Cowstails and Cobras II. Dubuque, IA: Kendall/Hunt and Project Adventure. (ISBN 08403-5434-7).

Rohnke, K. & Butler, S. (1995). QuickSilver. Dubuque, IA: Kendall/Hunt and Project Adventure. (ISBN 0-7872-0032-8).

Rohnke, K. (1991). The Bottomless Bag Again. Dubuque, IA: Kendall/Hunt. (ISBN 0-8403-8757-1).

Rohnke, K. (1998). Funn Stuff (vol. III). Dubuque, IA: Kendall/Hunt. (ISBN 0-7872-4654-9).

Rohnke, K. (1996). Funn Stuff (vol. II). Dubuque, IA: Kendall/Hunt. (ISBN 0-7872-2316-6).

Rohnke, K. (1996). Funn Stuff (vol. I). Dubuque, IA: Kendall/Hunt. (ISBN 0-7872-1633-X).

Rohnke, K. (1991). Bottomless Baggie. Dubuque, IA: Kendall/Hunt. (ISBN 0-8403-6813-5).

Rohnke, K. & Grout, J. (1998). Back Pocket Adventure. Needham Heights, MA: Simon & Schuster and Project Adventure. (ISBN 0-536-01419-1).

Sikes, S. (1995). Feeding the Zircon Gorilla. Tulsa, OK: Learning Unlimited. (ISBN 0-9646541-0-5).

Sikes, S. (1998). Executive Marbles. Tulsa, OK: Learning Unlimited. (ISBN 0-9646541-2-1).

Cavert, C. & Sikes, S. (1997). 50 Ways to Use Your Noodle. Tulsa, OK: Learning Unlimited. (ISBN 0-9646541-1-3).

Sanders, G. (1991). The Pictorial Guide to Group Work Activities. UK: author. (ISBN 0-9517302-0-7).

Simpson, B. (1974). Initiative Games. Butler, PA: author (ISBN not given).

Gass, M. A. (1995). Book of Metaphors (vol. II). Dubuque, IA: Kendall/Hunt. (ISBN 0-7872-0306-8).

Cain, J. & Joliff, B. (1998). Teamwork & Teamplay. Dubuque, IA: Kendall/Hunt. (ISBN 0-7872-4532-1).

Karl's Introduction

FUNN: Functional Understanding Not Necessary. This means there doesn't need to be a reason for having fun. As you are looking through these well defined and often resolute initiative situations, I'd suggest a light facilitating touch. The military drill instructor's purposes and techniques, although admittedly effective in context, are not what you are looking for. These initiative activities are designed to allow for a maximum of chosen challenge and an equally large dose of individual and group decision making. Solid bottom line goals occur most frequently when the fun quotient rides high. So, if the question is asked why the group's performance capability seems as high as the ongoing fun factor, refer to the acronym above, nod, smile knowingly, and resist the temptation to formulate a serious response.

SAFETY: Can a program be too safe? Our lives are buttressed with safety, mothers, insurance programs, eating right, exercise, home security, etc. However, the answer is yes. Not only can you be too safe, but you can also suffocate the adventure of a program with safety. The rather-safe-than-sorry commitment is often a difficult curriculum offender to recognize or criticize, but everything one does is safe, stultifyingly safe. The danger of being too safe (an oxymoronic phrase of profound proportion) is the insidious attrition of perceived risk (emotional and/or physical risk). Part of the recognized validity of play is the perceived risk; as the spark of risk is reduced, so is the satisfaction of participation and achievement. Recognize that you are dealing with adults who make their own safety decisions on a regular basis, and that you are presenting program segments that are well tested. Don't overwhelm participants with a blanket of security; that's what mothers are for. Also, it's difficult to maintain a go-for-it approach when your presentation is peppered with caveats. By all means remove hazardous obstacles, stop dangerous horseplay, and move activities to less perilous locations. Be safe, but don't flout it!

DISCLAIMER: Most of the activities detailed in this book can be utilized without technical training. However, some of the trust activities (#27, #28, etc.) need special training and practice to be accomplished and facilitated safely. Be overt by being baffled by the covert, get some friendly help. All authors, activity originators, and publishers accept no responsibility or liability for how you choose to interpret and employ these activities. Be careful and thoughtful. Understand that the improper use of these activities can lead to serious injury and death!

Lastly, I'd like to thank Simon for his hard work on the business introductions that accompany each activity. No one says you have to do every one of them this way, but if you keep the corporate context, the activities should mean more to your clients and that will likely lead to a more effective program of learning and change.

The Authors

Simon Priest, Ph.D. is the leading researcher and writer in the area of corporate experiential training and development. He presently consults for a handful of progressive corporations interested in staying ahead of their global competition by focusing on the acquisition and maintenance of relationships among human resources. His consulting expertise lies in facilitation, leadership and executive programs.

Karl Rohnke is a name synonymous with group initiatives and ropes courses. His best selling books and pioneering designs set the innovative standards of this field. He currently travels worldwide, presenting clinics on the application of experiential activities to all kinds of human growth situations. He has written over a dozen books devoted to active-based learning and adventure activities.

Key Definitions

The 101 activities in this book comprise one form of action events that are used in experiential training and development programs around the world. **Experiential training and development** is the purposeful use of active experiences to enhance organizational change through employee learning. Often this employee learning takes place in groups and involves the development of teamwork. Here lies the value of these 101 activities.

This form of training and development is experiential because elements of action, reflection, transfer and support are consciously added to the experience. **Action** means that the experience involves the doing (active) rather than the being done to (passive). **Reflection** examines the process of an experience, enhances awareness of learning and highlights changes in feeling, thinking or behaving that derive from that experience. **Transfer** occurs when change from the experiential program shows up in the workplace (transfer can be enhanced by using metaphoric imagery). **Support**, through a chance to practice with time and resources at work, encourages one to continue learning, maintain change, and lessen resistance. While activities form the action phase of this four step cycle, the other three are achieved through facilitation techniques, especially with a debriefing discussion after each activity.

Glossary of Terms

A few key words are used repeatedly throughout the book and are explained here in alphabetical order.

Belaying is the correct use of a rope and friction devices to protect against a person falling from considerable height (like on a ropes course or climbing wall). Belaying is NOT necessary for any activities in this book; however, spotting should be used as the chosen form of protection for many of these activities.

Bumpers-up is the term given to placing hands up in front of oneself when walking blindfolded. In this way, one's hands bump into any unexpected obstacle rather than the rest of one's body. The position for bumpers-up is arms extended forward, with palms up at about face level, and elbows bent at right angles while tucked into the body above the hips. Bumpers-up is not the same as spotting.

Challenge by choice emphasizes that clients are the ones who determine the extent of their involvement in any activity. It means that individuals have the right to choose their level of participation. Full participation is doing everything in an activity. Partial may involve lifting and not being lifted, or visa versa. Non-participation means observing. Observers have a valuable role to play in reporting their observations back to the group during the debrief. Any facilitators who coerce or force clients to participate against their wills are acting unethically and irresponsibly.

Consequences are those handicapping penalties measured out by facilitators when rules are violated during activities. Although these are recommended for each activity, facilitators are free to not apply consequences or to change the consequences (as long as they clearly state this in advance) to some of these: starting over, blindfolding, muting, breaking or slinging limbs, reducing time, losing equipment, limiting attempts, changing places, and becoming an observer.

Spotting is the preventive act of protecting a person in a fall during an activity. Falls should be anticipated any time a person is above ground level and spotters should be used accordingly. Spotting softens a fall, not stops it! Although spotting techniques may vary among activities, the general principle is the same: protect the upper body (especially the head and shoulders) of the falling person. Do NOT attempt to catch the individual as this can lead to injuries for the spotter. Spotters are a support system to be used whenever necessary. They are not meant to aid or interfere with a person's progress during an activity. In order to spot, spotters should place one foot in front of the other (about shoulder width apart), with their knees slightly bent (to protect their lower back), arms up, fingers together, with their hands directed toward the head or shoulders of a potential faller, and with their eyes attentive to all movement by that person. Spotters follow along with the person, gauging changes in balance, height or momentum and adjusting their own positions accordingly. Don't expect a faller to come to the spotter!

Warm-ups are exercises done prior to the program. After a break, and before starting any activities, encourage people to stretch and move around (raising their heart rates slightly, but not to the point of sweating). For added safety, this is also the time to have them remove jewelry (such as rings or earrings), clothing (belt buckle or heavy jacket), or any sharp objects in their pockets (such as pens or pencils) that might scratch themselves or others.

Facilitation

Facilitation is anything done before, during or after the experience (activity) to enhance reflection, transfer, and support of learning and change. For example, the group debriefing (a discussion held after the experience) may allow group members to share their common reflections, transfer their lessons learned to work, and support one another in making future changes gained from their initial experience. Some of the more powerful and the most effective facilitation techniques include: funneling; frontloading; framing; and solution-focused approaches.

Funneling is a structured form of debriefing where questions are asked and sequenced in a deliberate pattern. In most debriefings, the facilitator will ask a few questions and the discussion will ramble on and/or go off on tangents. This is an appropriate discovery method to find out what was learned. However, funneling is a more confirmatory method to cement what is changing. The questions follow this general sequence of six:

> REVIEW: Can you review the order of things that happened in the last activity?
> RECALL-REMEMBER: Do you recall an example of poor or good (<u>put topic here</u>)?
> AFFECT-EFFECT: What was the impact of this occurrence on you, the group or task?
> SUMMATION: Can you sum up what you have learned from all this discussion so far?
> APPLICATION: How does the important lesson you learned relate to your life or work?
> COMMITMENT: What will you do differently in the next activity or upon return to work?

Frontloading is asking questions (normally reserved for the debrief) in advance of the experience as a means to punctuate learning and bring change in the midst of the experience (as opposed to later on after a debrief). Used about 10% of the time, and only when necessary to emphasize change, frontloading questions take five forms:

REVISITING: Who can remind us about the behaviors we agreed to improve for this next activity?

OBJECTIVES: What do you think that this activity is designed to teach you or the group?

MOTIVATION: How might this learning be utilized in your regular life or on the daily job?

FUNCTION: What are positive actions necessary to succeed and how can they be increased?

DYSFUNCTION: What are negative actions that bring failure and how can they be decreased?

Framing is the way in which each activity is introduced. Four possible types of frames are:

FANTASY or the fairy tale introduction that includes items like: spiders, sharks, alligators, poison peanut butter, radioactive yogurt, nitroglycerin, TNT, corrosive acid, floods, and forest fires.

REALITY or the what-you-see-is-what-you-get introduction where items are called by their actual name: planks, ropes, grassy areas, trees, barrels, buckets, bricks, balls, and blindfolds.

CONTEXTUAL or a general business introduction where items have connection to the corporate context: call center, human resources, finances, accounting, information technology, marketing, and customer service. Contextual framing is used for most activity introductions in this book.

ISOMORPHIC is the use of specific metaphors that fit perfectly and uniquely for different clients. Isomorph means the same structure and requires that elements (props, consequences, rewards, or outcomes) of the activity be introduced in a way that creates a metaphor for each client and that is special for their culture only. It is more than just changing the names like in contextual framing.

Solution-focused facilitation is a reversal of the problem-focused approach facilitators normally use. Problem-focused facilitators investigate what is wrong with the group, what causes their problem, when and where it occurs, why it has continued to be a problem, and how they can try harder to fix or overcome it. Solution-focused facilitation does not ignore a presenting problem, but strives to bring about its resolution by helping clients to identify, construct, and implement solutions to that problem.

In this approach, facilitation centers around: identifying what clients want (solutions) rather than what they don't want (problems); looking for what is currently working for clients rather than what is not; emphasizing what clients are doing already that is useful (stressing client strengths); and assisting clients in doing something different (solutions) instead of investing in something that isn't working for them (problems). Solution-focused facilitators look for exceptions to the problem (when or where it doesn't occur or investigating why it doesn't happen) and establishes how clients can work differently at another solution, rather than harder at the same problem, to accomplish more lasting change.

For more information on learning how to facilitate with these advanced methods, see <u>Essential Elements of Facilitation</u>, by Priest, Gass & Gillis and available from TARRAK Technologies:

www.tarrak.com
info@tarrak.com

Table of Activities

No.	Activity Name	Prop	Move	Time	Size
1	Name Communication	1	1	5-10	10-20
2	Messaging System	2	1	10-20	10-20
3	High Speed Data Transfer	1	1	20-30	10-20
4	Crux Identification	2	0	5-10	10-20
5	Problem Solving	1	1	10-30	5-20
6	Problem or Solution	0	2	5-30	5-15
7	Sharing Resources	1	1	30-60	6-12
8	Integration vs. Separation	1	1	20-30	8-10
9	Minimizing Waste	1	1	10-30	10-20
10	Competing for Resources	1	1	10-30	10-100
11	Elevating the Corporation	2	2	20-40	5-10
12	Life: A Balancing Act	2	0	10-20	10-20
13	Office Wiring, etc.	0	0	10-20	10-20
14	Reorganizing Inventory	1	0	10-20	5-10
15	Passwords & Combinations	1	1	20-30	9-25
16	Raising Group Performance	1	3	10-30	2-20
17	Serving Customers	2	2	10-20	10-100
18	Hiring Staff to Fit the Job	2	0	10-20	2-100
19	Reorganizing the Hierarchy	1	1	20-30	2-20
20	Supporting your Leader	1	1	20-30	10-30
21	Product Packaging	2	1	30-60	3-10
22	Reaching the Sales Quota	1	1	20-30	3-20
23	Partners for Work	1	2	10-20	2-20
24	Travelling in Foreign Lands	1	2	20-40	5-20
25	Sharing a Common Vision	1	2	10-30	5-20
26	Group Trust & Support	1	2	5-10	10-100
27	Mutual Trust & Support	0	3	10-30	6-12
28	Coworker Trust & Support	4	4	30-60	8-12
29	Completing Projects	1	0	10-30	7-21
30	Replicating from Blueprints	2	1	20-30	5-15
31	Disassembly & Reassembly	2	1	30-60	10-20
32	Building a New Structure	2	2	30-60	5-10
33	Shaping the Organization	2	1	10-30	4-40

No.	Activity Name	Prop	Move	Time	Size
34	Product Logo Duplication	1	1	10-20	5-10
35	Producing a Prototype	2	1	30-60	10-20
36	Factory Pilot Testing	3	2	60-120	10-50
37	Project Setbacks	2	1	20-40	2-20
38	Getting There on Time	1	2	10-20	10-30
39	Organization Orientation	1	3	20-40	5-40
40	Competing for Customers	2	3	20-30	10-40
41	Caring for Customers	2	1	5-10	5-20
42	Warehouse Inventory	1	3	20-40	10-30
43	Smooth Shift Changes	1	2	10-30	10-40
44	What Do You Stand For?	0	1	5-30	5-100
45	Project Management	4	2	10-30	6-12
46	World Journey	4	2	20-40	8-16
47	Restructuring the Company	1	2	10-30	5-20
48	Corporate Mergers	1	2	20-40	10-40
49	Group Golf	3	2	120-240	4-16
50	Saving Stranded Motorists	3	2	30-60	5-10
51	Removing Waste Products	3	1	30-60	5-15
52	Winning Back Customers	3	3	30-60	5-15
53	Accessing Archived Data	3	3	30-90	5-15
54	Building a Network	2	3	30-90	5-10
55	Computer Disinfectant	2	2	30-60	10-20
56	Obtaining Raw Materials	2	2	20-40	5-10
57	Disseminating Supplies	3	2	20-40	5-10
58	Conveyer Systems	3	2	30-60	5-15
59	Goods to the Warehouse	2	2	20-40	2-10
60	Delivering to Market	3	1	30-60	5-10
61	Sampling Public Opinion	4	2	30-60	5-10
62	Plugging Leaks with P.R.	2	2	20-40	10-20
63	Aquaducts/Oil Pipelines	2	1	10-30	5-50
64	Shipping by Rail	2	1	10-30	5-50
65	Trucking to the Showroom	2	3	30-60	5-10
66	Transitioning toward Profit	3	3	30-60	5-10
67	Acquiring New Customers	3	3	20-40	2-15

No.	Activity Name	Prop	Move	Time	Size
68	Surviving the Fiscal Year	1	2	20-40	5-15
69	New Mission Statement	3	3	20-40	5-10
70	Shepherding the Proposal	2	3	30-60	5-25
71	One for All and All for One!	1	4	20-40	10-25
72	Everyone for Themselves!	2	2	20-40	5-15
73	Quality Is a Journey	1	1	30-60	5-20
74	Gather a Group Together	3	4	60-120	10-20
75	Data Download	1	4	20-40	5-30
76	Conflict Resolution	3	4	30-90	5-15
77	Distribution Network	3	4	30-90	5-20
78	Labor Negotiations	3	3	30-90	10-20
79	Executing a Strategic Plan	3	2	30-60	5-10
80	Insured Objectives	4	3	30-90	5-15
81	Partner Trust & Support	4	3	30-60	2-10
82	Trading Places	4	2	30-60	10-20
83	Replacing a Defective Part	4	4	30-60	5-20
84	Constant Patient Care	4	4	30-60	5-20
85	Wholesale to Retail	4	4	30-60	5-20
86	Insurmountable Obstacles	4	4	30-60	5-20
87	Ascending to a New Order	4	4	30-60	5-20
88	Courier Delivery	3	3	30-60	5-15
89	Corporate Ladder Climbing	2	4	10-20	5-10
90	Making Defect-free Widgets	2	2	30-60	10-100
91	Group that Blows Together	2	1	30-60	5-10
92	Building a Better Mousetrap	2	1	30-60	5-10
93	Target Audience	2	1	30-60	5-10
94	Quality Benchmarking	2	1	30-60	5-10
95	Seamless Programming	2	1	30-60	10-20
96	Workforce Integration	4	4	60-120	10-40
97	Passenger Transportation	3	3	60-120	10-20
98	Hostile Takeover	3	2	60-120	20-100
99	Collecting Outstanding Debt	4	3	120-240	10-100
100	Search & Rescue	4	4	240-480	10-100
101	The Final Problem	3	3	240-480	10-100

Activities Legend

Information for each activity is presented in a consistent format. These pages explain the typical information presented. Each activity is named and numbered (from 1 to 101). Higher numbered activities tend to be more complex, require more PROPS or facilities, and demand more MOVEment or action, according to these two scales:

PROPS: 0 = none
     1 = only one prop
     2 = two or more props
     3 = unique setup or layout
     4 = specially constructed facility

MOVEment: 0 = none / sitting
     1 = light / standing
     2 = medium / walking
     3 = heavy / sweating
     4 = extreme / lifting

Other summarized information includes TIME taken to complete the action (does not include time for debriefing), recommended group SIZE (range of upper and lower limits), ALIAS (an activity's common name with reference to page numbers in the books listed in Simon's Introduction), and ORIGIN (with credit to the inventors).

No.   Name of the Activity

PROPS: **TIME:**   **ALIAS:**
MOVE: **SIZE:**   **ORIGIN:**

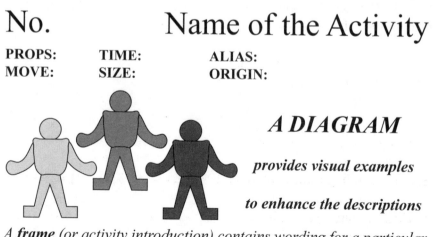

A DIAGRAM

provides visual examples

to enhance the descriptions

*A **frame** (or activity introduction) contains wording for a particular business context (see framing on page 9). Obviously these frames will not suit all groups, so change these in the best interests of your clients. These introductions are written as facilitators speak: in first person and with metaphors (actual items are given in parentheses).*

Action generally describes what the group will be doing during the team-building activity.

Intent lists a few of the learning outcomes that may be obtained from the activity. These are worthwhile topics for later debriefing.

Note presents important information, cautions or considerations about the activity before you proceed.

Equipment is a list of the props, consumable supplies and special facilities needed to conduct the activity.

Setup describes the steps taken to prepare for the activity: how to layout the area and distribute the equipment.

Task is a specific summary of what the group is expected to do in order to accomplish its goal for that activity.

Constraints are the rules that purposefully restrict or hamper a group in its efforts to succeed or achieve its goal.

Safety points out some, not all, considerations for protecting clients from common physical injuries. You are responsible for all safety.

Facilitation includes a few tips and tricks to aid the facilitator (see pages 8-10 for more ideas). A number of likely solutions are explained, so you know what to expect from successful groups. Some debriefing topics are given beyond the intended items above.

Variations suggests some alterations that make the activity easier, harder, or just plain different.

The DIAGRAM that enhances the above descriptions with visual examples, also shows the activity setup, action, solution or gear.

1   **Name Communication**

PROPS: 1   **TIME:**   5-10   **ALIAS:** Toss a Name, SB-17
MOVE: 1   **SIZE:**   10-20   **ORIGIN:** Classic

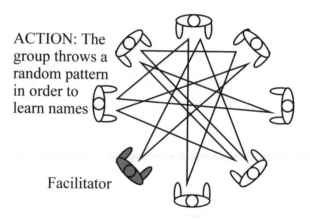

ACTION: The group throws a random pattern in order to learn names

Facilitator

This activity will help me (and perhaps you) to get to know each other's names. First, let's go around the circle a couple of times <u>slowly</u> and have everyone take a turn to <u>clearly</u> announce the name they would like to use today. I'll start: my name is.... Now that we've heard all of our names, I'd like you to pick some one to send this message to (hold up the throwing object). As with any communication process, you will need to establish a link by calling out their name and by making eye contact with them before you <u>gently</u> send a message. Once you receive the message from someone, you want to provide clear feedback by saying thank you and stating the name of the person who sent the message (before sending the message on to another person). Any questions? If you forget people's names, like I often do, don't worry or feel the need to apologize, just ask. Let's go!

Action: Participants stand in a circle and toss an object from person to person while learning each other's names.

Intent: Familiarization with group members' names and examination of effective communication models.

Note: While this is essentially an icebreaker for group members who do not know one another at all, it can also be used as a lead-in to the next two activities, even with familiar groups.

Equipment: One soft throwable object (like a fleece ball, rubber chicken, squeaky toy, or flexible frisbee).

Setup: Gather the group and join with them in a circle, standing at least arm's length apart.

Task: Learn the names of everyone in the group, by throwing an object to them and calling out their names.

Constraints: None, but there is no rule that says everyone must learn every single name. Let the group choose.

Safety: Discourage throws that are dangerous, hard or wild. Remind folks to make eye contact before throwing.

Facilitation: This is one of the few activities where the facilitator is actually a part of the group. If the next two activities are used in a program, take the opportunity to slowly and successively move apart from the group. For a debrief, stay with the communication metaphor and discuss the reasons why some messages were not received (dropped).

Variations: For groups who know every member's names, new nicknames or alliterations (like Safety Simon or Krazy Karl) can be made up and used for the program. Sillier throwing objects tend to relax people. Once names are fairly well known, ask people to step backwards and widen the circle, or introduce several new objects, which can lead into group juggling (see activity #2). Split large groups into several smaller ones and occasionally take a break from the action to mix people among groups, then let people change groups when they are ready to meet others. Encourage people to vary the kind of throws they use (like over the head, under the leg, with a side foot kick, but not high speed pitches). If objects are not available, ask people to pass handshakes or similar greetings.

2   Messaging System

PROPS: 2   **TIME:** 10-20   **ALIAS:** Group Juggling, CC-84
MOVE: 1   **SIZE:** 10-20   **ORIGIN:** Karl Rohnke

ACTION: The group repeatedly throws the same pattern in order to establish a sequence

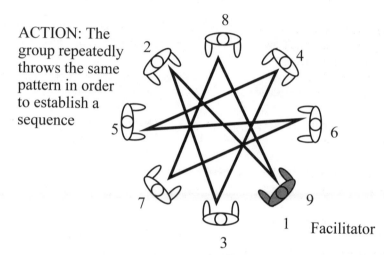

Now I have one message (throwable object) that everyone needs to share in a particular sequence. To establish this sequence, I'd like everyone to assume the catching position (demonstrate elbows at the side, forearms level and hands up with palms extended). This will signify that you are ready to receive the message. Once you have this message, and have passed it on to someone who has not yet received it, you may stand normally. This will tell us who have been contacted and who has yet to be reached. I'll start the message on its way around the group and, after it has touched everyone, it should come back to finish with me for the very last communication. Any questions? Let's practice.... Now that we have established our sequence, let's see how many messages our system can handle (begin sending objects into the sequence in an almost metronome fashion until the maximum limit is reached -- repeat as needed). If we drop messages, simply retrieve them and continue.

Action: Multiple objects flying about in all directions with the group frantically trying to keep it all together.

Intent: Quantity versus quality, systems thinking, and communication.

Note: This activity can be done without establishing the sequence described below, but the sequence aids with transition into the next activity (#3). Some groups have greater success without being restricted by a sequence.

Equipment: Several soft throwable objects (like fleece balls, rubber chickens, squeaky toys & flexible frisbees).

Setup: While still standing as part of the circle from the previous activity, begin to introduce several new objects.

Task: To see how many objects the group can maintain in play for a set number of throws without dropping any.

Constraints: Any dropped objects need to be retrieved and reintroduced into the system as quickly as possible.

Safety: A common group goal is one object per member being passed around, but don't let this zeal for numbers compromise safety. Be sure to remind people about the importance of soft objects, gentle throws, and eye contact.

Facilitation: During the chaos, ask a couple of questions like "Is this feeling like work?" or "What gets juggled at the office?" Discuss quantity versus quality issues that might arise. Ask if there was ever a time when more objects were on the ground than in the air. Avoid comparing this group's performance with that of other groups.

Variations: Substitute objects of consequence (raw eggs or water balloons). Expand the diameter of the circle.

3   High Speed Data Transfer

PROPS: 1 **TIME:** 20-30 **ALIAS:** Warp Speed, CC-83
MOVE: 1 **SIZE:** 10-20 **ORIGIN:** Karl Rohnke

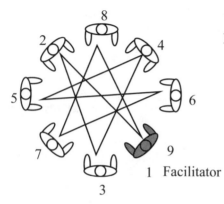

FIRST ORDER CHANGE
tighten the system & work harder

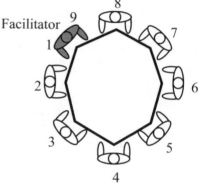

SECOND ORDER CHANGE
restructure the existing system

VARIOUS
SOLUTIONS

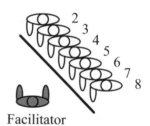

THIRD ORDER CHANGE
restructure for a new system

In our last activity, we went for volume. Here, transfer speed is important. Using our sequence, I'm interested in seeing how fast we can pass this information (object) so that everyone receives it independently and in the correct order. Any questions? Would someone with a stopwatch (midway in the sequence) please time our performance? Okay, GO!... Now, that was a pretty good time, but in the interest of quality improvement, I challenge this group to transfer the data throughout the group in half that time. Let's try again.... Now I'm interested in whether you can get done in under 10 seconds!... 5 seconds!!... ONE SECOND!!!...

Action: Throwing a soft object in sequence from person-to-person as quickly and efficiently as possible.

Intent: Systems thinking, restructuring systems, and quantity versus quality.

Note: This is probably the last of these activities in which the facilitator would function as part of the group.

Equipment: One soft throwable object (like a fleece ball, rubber chicken, squeaky toy, or flexible frisbee).

Setup: While standing as part of the circle from the previous activity, the facilitator prepares to leave the circle.

Task: To pass the object (following the sequence from person to person) in increasingly shorter time periods.

Constraints: Everyone must contact the object, and everyone must contact it in order of the previous sequence. Time starts when the object begins its journey from the facilitator and ends when it returns back to that facilitator. No penalties for a dropped object (except the obvious loss of time to pick it up and reintroduce it to the system). The object cannot be held by one person while being touched by the others. People may change positions.

Safety: Groups may come up with unusual and creative approaches, so veto any actions that seem unsafe. The usual progression of change is to tighten the sequenced circle (< 30 secs.), reorganize the circle by standing in the order of the sequence (< 10 secs.), build a ramp of hands (< 5 secs.), build a ramp of fingers (< 1 sec.), etc.

Facilitation: Groups typically restrict their thinking to first order change: doing things the same way, just better and faster. They simply try to pass the ball back and forth as quickly as they can. At some point, they may shift to second order change: doing things differently and easier. They may reorganize themselves in the same circle, but stand next to the people they receive from and send to. When challenged with a seemingly impossible goal (1 second), they may abandon the circle in favor of a new system and demonstrate third order change. Debrief this in relation to systems thinking and restructuring. Discuss the tradeoffs in terms of lost data or diminished quality.

Variations: For greater difficulty, this can be done with multiple objects passed in a precise order of reception.

4   Crux Identification

PROPS: 2   **TIME:**   5-10   **ALIAS:** 2B or Knot 2B, TT-60
MOVE: 0   **SIZE:**   10-20 **ORIGIN:** Jim Cain, Rubik's Tangle

SETUP

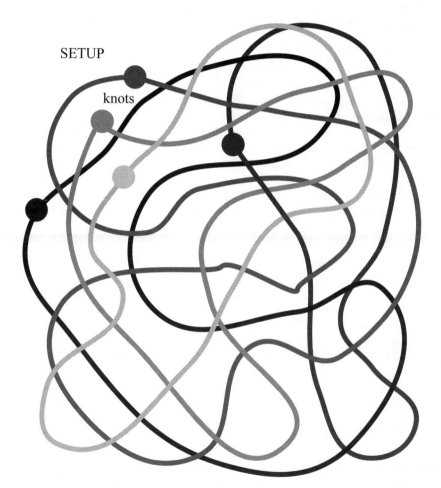

knots

In front of you is a big problem (collection of loops) made up from a number of little problems (each knotted loop). As is often the case with big problems, solving the initial key crux problem often leads to solving the rest of the problem. Without actually modifying the problem in anyway (don't touch anything), your task is to discover and agree on which of the composite problems is holding the entire problem together. Any questions?

Action: Group examines a series of loops and knots and attempts to agree on which are linked and which aren't.

Intent: Consensus building, negotiation, problem solving, decision making, communication, and sharing ideas.

Note: This works best with 5 loops: more (6 or 7) provide greater difficulty and fewer (3 or 4) give greater ease.

Equipment: Several short pieces of cord about 10' long and in different colors (substitute rope or shoelaces).

Setup: Tie all the cords into loops with a variety of knots (overhand, granny, or water). Tie the last loop so that it connects the other loops (last cord gets passed through the centers of all the other loops before getting knotted). Spread the collection of connected loops out on the ground so that the single encompassing loop is not obvious.

Task: Group must reach consensus on which one of the connected loops holds all the other loops together.

Constraints: You cannot move, touch, untangle, or unravel any of the cords or knots.

Safety: Ask people to take care to avoid tripping over the cords, if these are widely spread out.

Facilitation: This is a good opportunity to examine how ideas are shared and listened to by the group. Discuss how the final decision was reached and whether the group conformed to the general principles of consensus or followed another method (democratic vote or coercive tactics). Did they try to discover which was the right one or eliminate the ones that were not? What means did they use to check that their choice was correct?

Variations: Use extremely long ropes and spread them out over a large area and repeatedly twist them around one another to give the illusion of connectivity. Make all the cords the same color (or the same color and pattern) for more confusion. Substitute knots for loops, and present a series of tangles (some tied and others not) and ask "which of these cords will form into knots if pulled at both ends and which will not?" (Not Knots in TT-142).

5 **Problem Solving**

PROPS: 1 **TIME:** 10-30 **ALIAS:** Knots in a Rope, FSI-27
MOVE: 1 **SIZE:** 5-20 **ORIGIN:** Karl Rohnke

SETUP: One starting position

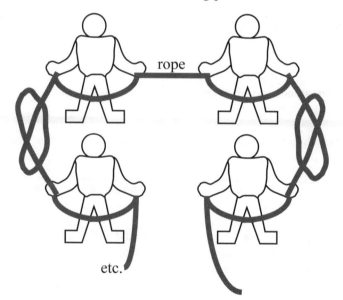

rope

etc.

This program is about teamwork and one place that teamwork is needed is in solving multiple problems. You are holding multiple problems (several knots in the rope) and are charged with the challenge of solving these (untying the knots) without letting the problem get away from you (don't let go of the rope). Any questions?

Action: While acting as part of the rope, group members untie and tie knots in the rope.

Intent: Cooperation, communication, trust, problem solving, and spatial thinking.

Note: Instead of one long continuous rope, several short pieces can be substituted and held person to person.

Equipment: One long continuous piece of rope (at least 3' of length for each person in the group).

Setup: Tie several overhand knots in the rope (one knot for every two people in the group) and lay it down on the floor. Ask everyone to grab the rope with one or both hands and spread out in a long straight line.

Task: To untie several knots in a rope without letting go of the rope.

Constraints: Hands may slide along the rope, but may not let go of it (preclude sliding for more difficulty).

Safety: Sometimes people get contorted into awkward situations. Watch for this and do spotting as necessary.

Facilitation: Spatial problems like these are extremely difficult for some groups. Be prepared to discuss rising levels of frustration or dealing with failure. Debrief for general teamwork, cooperation, or communication.

Variations: Once the knots are undone, have the group retie them. Try more complex knots like a figure 8 or a bowline). Have one facilitator be the shoe and ask the group to tie a shoelace bow around that facilitator.

6   **Problem or Solution**

PROPS: 0 **TIME:** 5-30 **ALIAS:** Human Knots, SB-117
MOVE: 2 **SIZE:** 5-15 **ORIGIN:** Classic

ACTION: A partially
untangled Human
Knot

Sometimes we are a part of a problem without knowing it and sometimes we are so close to the problem that we can't help solve it. Solve this problem (untangle your human knot) without walking away or looking at it from a distance (don't break contact) and without telling others what they must do (no talking). Any questions?

Action: The group is holding hands, inextricably entwined in a large knot, and working to become disentangled.

Intent: Trust, cooperation, communication, problem solving, and spatial thinking.

Note: This activity requires some potentially sweaty hand holding and some tight positions in close proximity. If these are concerns, then ask participants to hold scarves or short rope segments between their hands instead.

Equipment: None (unless substituting scarves or short ropes).

Setup: Have the group gather in a circle, standing shoulder to shoulder. Ask them to raise their right hand and grab the right hand of a person across the circle from them. Then, ask them to repeat this with their left hand, but NOT to grab the hands of the same person. If two people are holding both of one another's hands, they are their own isolated circle, so ask them to find new partners for at least one of the linkages. The result is a human knot. To check this knot is continuous, have one person pass an impulse around the group by squeezing only one hand.

Task: Untangle the human knot, without talking or releasing grips, to create one or more circles of people.

Constraints: Don't let go of hands. Rotate or pivot grips as required to ease movement. No talking.

Safety: Spot people who must step over others, balance on one foot, or place themselves at similar risk.

Facilitation: For groups that get stuck and show no hope of getting unstuck, offer Knot First Aid. Allow the group to break one linkage in order to succeed and then encourage them to repeat one more attempt.

Variations: For really large groups, do the setup in small groups and then break one link in each group and connect all the groups back together into one big group again. The use of short rope segments makes this easier.

7   Sharing Resources

PROPS: 1   **TIME:**   30-60   **ALIAS:** Traffic Jam, SB-122
MOVE: 1   **SIZE:**   6-12   **ORIGIN:** Classic

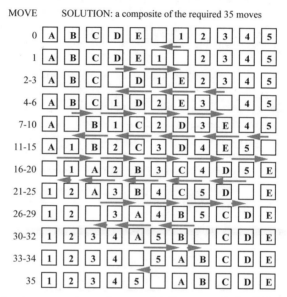

MOVE   SOLUTION: a composite of the required 35 moves

In most organizations, people work toward different goals by different means, but with shared rules and resources. Here are two sides attempting to reach their goals (change places) by sharing resources (spaces) and following the same rules. You have ten collective attempts before bankruptcy. Don't leave your existing resource (space), except to move forward (never backwards) into an unoccupied resource (into an empty space). You may move around only one (never more) of the other side (and never anyone on your side) and only one person at a time can move toward their goal. Breaking a rule costs 10% of your funding and you start over. Any questions? Here is a review of the rules....

1. You can only move forward (you can't move backwards).
2. You must remain on a space (you can't step off to have a discussion).
3. You can only move into open spaces (can't occupy spaces that others are on).
4. You can only move around a person from the opposite side into the next open space (can't move around your own side's members).
5. You can only move around one person at a time (can't move around two or more people who block you).
6. Only one person may move at a time (two or more people can't move simultaneously).

Action: Two equal halves of a group attempt to change places by taking turns to move according to several rules.

Intent: Incidental and accidental competition, cooperation, communication, trust, and problem solving.

Note: This is one of few activities that has a single answer and requires an even number of people to perform. Ask odd numbers to volunteer a single observer.

Equipment: Several spaces (carpet squares or paper sheets), one for each person (even numbers of people) plus one extra (making for an odd number of spaces).

Setup: Place the odd number of spaces in a line and stand on the center space. Invite group members to occupy the remaining even number of spaces and ask them to turn to face you in the middle. Then step off the middle space.

Task: To change places with one's corresponding cross partner (A-1, B-2, C-3, etc.) without breaking any rules.

Constraints: The six basic rules are summarized opposite. Breaking a rule requires you to start over with the loss of one of your limited number of tries.

Safety: If people look like they will lose their balance from treading carefully, then permit temporary step offs.

Facilitation: Sometimes facilitators can forget the necessary moves (only one solution will work). This is okay, because revealing the answer might be inappropriate rescuing behavior. Simply ask the group to work on it later. Sometimes groups accidentally stumble on the answer, but have no idea how they did it. Ask them to replicate their solution in the opposite direction starting from where they ended up. The trick to finding and remembering a solution lies in this hint: once a side begins to move, everyone on that side moves unless a move puts one person behind another person from the same side (avoid doing this since it makes a two person block against the other side). Interesting discussion topics include how a side's eagerness to succeed can block the other's progress.

Variations: To make this activity easier, or permit more discussion, lay the line of spaces in a curve. Consider adding non-verbal constraints or letting the group step away from the problem in order to plan better. As the number of people on each side increases, the task gets more complex, consider splitting groups in half and putting their two lines in a cross (+) with a shared empty space to start (which will fill to block one group, once the other group begins to move).

8   Integration vs. Separation

PROPS: 1   **TIME:** 20-30   **ALIAS:** 2x4 or 4x2, SB-123
MOVE: 1   **SIZE:** 8-10   **ORIGIN:** Classic

MOVE   SOLUTION: a composite of the required 4 moves

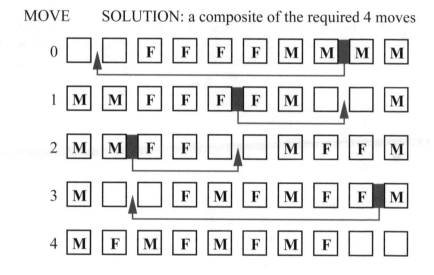

Your group represents a separated community where cliques exist (males together and females together). Your task is to integrate your community so that no one stands beside anyone from their same clique (alternating males and females). Since change is always a little uncomfortable and in order to support the changes made, no one will be asked to reposition on their own and must do so with the accompaniment of a partner (move pairs of adjacent people). As partners change, they cannot switch relative positions (once a pair moves they can't change places). Stay with your present position until you have a chance to change (stay on your space until your turn comes) and when you change, only take a position that is already unoccupied (move to open spaces only). Any questions?

Action: Pairs changing spaces to rearrange the entire group according to a set of rules.

Intent: Diversity, cooperation, communication, problem solving, and leadership.

Note: This is a good alternative to the previous activity (which may already be known or may be solved quickly).

Equipment: Ten spaces (carpet squares or paper sheets) and 8 people (for example: 4 males and 4 females).

Setup: Lay out 10 spaces in a line. Ask males to stand beside one another on 4 spaces and females beside them together on the next 4 spaces, with the 2 end spaces left open. Substitute colors of clothes if genders are unequal.

Task: Rearrange the group from a separated (M M M M F F F F) to an integrated (M F M F M F M F) sequence.

Constraints: You must remain on your spaces and you can only move into open spaces. You must move in pairs (a pair is any two adjacent people and these pairs may change). Moving pairs must stay in their orientation (changing places in mid-move cannot be used to gain an advantage). A move sideways is considered a full move.

Safety: If people look like they will lose their balance from treading carefully, then permit temporary step offs.

Facilitation: Ask non-participating others to watch and report their observations during the debrief. Encourage groups to hone their performance toward four paired moves (the minimum limit). Sometimes groups can accidentally stumble on the answer, but have no idea how they did it. Ask them to reverse their solution from integration to separation. Debrief for typical teamwork topics and any work diversity issues that may arise.

Variations: To make this activity easier, or permit more discussion, lay the line of spaces in a curve. Consider adding non-verbal constraints or letting the group step away from the problem in order to plan better. Once solved, challenge the group to complete the entire solution in the time it takes to hold their collective breath.

9   **Minimizing Waste**

PROPS: 1   **TIME:** 10-30   **ALIAS:** Jump Out, BBA-114
MOVE: 1   **SIZE:** 10-20   **ORIGIN:** Karl Rohnke

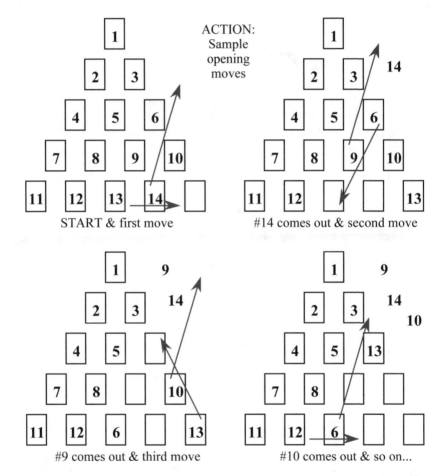

ACTION:
Sample
opening
moves

START & first move

#14 comes out & second move

#9 comes out & third move

#10 comes out & so on...

In this activity, we are interested in reducing existing waste to the bare minimum. Each of you represent unnecessary waste that will need to be eliminated from the system. The elimination of waste is accomplished by an efficiency audit process (jumping over someone into an open space). Eliminated waste (stands on the sidelines and) may still contribute valuable information to improve the audit process. This efficiency auditing will need to be repeated as often as possible until the absolute minimum waste (of a single person) is left. Any questions?

Action: Participants attempt to jump from space to space and successfully remove each other from the game.

Intent: Planning ahead, learning from failure, cooperation, communication, and problem solving.

Note: The triangle must be formed with 10, 15, 21, 28, 36, 45, 55 or 66 spaces. Select the nearest number of spaces greater than the group size. Extra spaces are okay, but the ideal is to begin with only one open space.

Equipment: Fifteen spaces (carpet squares or paper sheets) for a group of ten to fourteen people.

Setup: Arrange the spaces in a triangle, ask people to step onto their own space and leave only one space open.

Task: To reduce the group size to one member by removing others from the triangle by checker jumping them.

Constraints: You can only move into an open space by jumping over one adjacent teammate at a time. Stay on your space (one per person) unless jumping and only move by jumping. Teammates who get jumped must step off their space and stand to the side of the triangle, where they may continue to contribute to the solution. When no more jumps are possible, count how many people are left, and start again until only one person remains.

Safety: If people look like they will lose their balance from treading carefully, then permit temporary step offs.

Facilitation: Encourage learning from failure by permitting unlimited trial and error attempts. Since there are multiple variations on the solution, allow the group to discover their own best effort. Discuss planning ahead.

Variations: Try nonverbal for greater difficulty. Involve more people by having them stand in pairs (back to back) on the spaces to reduce conversation and encourage action. Vary the number of spaces and their shape.

10   **Competing for Resources**

PROPS: 1   **TIME:** 10-30   **ALIAS:** Tic Tac Toe, BPA-94
MOVE: 1   **SIZE:** 10-100   **ORIGIN:** Jim Grout

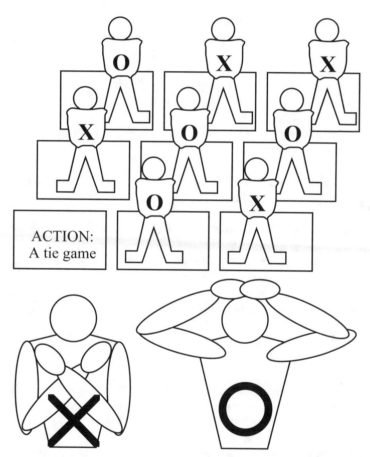

ACTION:
A tie game

Frequently, organizations have limited resources and have to make some tough decisions about who gets rewarded. Team X and Team O will take turns putting their members to work on one of 9 possible project components (these 9 spaces) in an effort to control three completed components in a row: (horizontally, vertically or diagonally like in a game of Tic Tac Toe). At the end of 20 such projects, the team with the highest success rate will receive the most resources. Any questions? Since you don't want the other group to know your strategy, this entire activity should be done nonverbally (without speaking even to your own group members).

Action: Two teams play the classic Tic Tac Toe game and several variations using themselves as the markers.

Intent: Competition versus cooperation, collaboration, communication, and problem solving.

Note: This is a more group-oriented and less physical alternative to the classic Candy Arm Wrestling, where two people are placed in the usual combative arrangement and told they get a candy reward each time they pin their opponent's hand. The real winners are the ones who take turns rapidly pinning one another in a spirit of cooperation and win bags of candy, while many others struggle and compete with their partners to get one piece.

Equipment: Nine spaces (carpet squares or paper sheets) for ten people. More spaces for the other variations.

Setup: Place the nine spaces on the floor in a 3 by 3 grid. Break the group of 10 in half (5 X's and 5 O's). Get them to practice making X by crossing their arms over their chest; or marking O by putting their hands on their head.

Task: To win at Tic Tac Toe by getting three of your people in a row up, down or diagonally on the board.

Constraints: Must be non-verbal. Teams take turns starting each game and then they take turns in the game.

Safety: Watch people's balance. If they crowd too closely together on the spaces, separate the spaces further.

Facilitation: Play this and keep score until both groups see the potentially adverse impact of competition within the organization and choose to either take turns winning and losing or to seek ties rather than a win-lose outcome. Discuss handling success and failure (win-lose or victory and defeat). Debrief cooperation versus competition. Differentiate between competition among groups within a corporation and competition between other companies.

Variations: Find a way to play this in three dimensions. If not, try a larger number of playing spaces (up to 10 by 10 to involve many more people) and require four or five people in a row to win a round.

11   Elevating the Corporation

PROPS: 2   **TIME:** 20-40   **ALIAS:** Suspension, FSIII-76
MOVE: 2   **SIZE:** 5-10   **ORIGIN:** Adrian Kissler

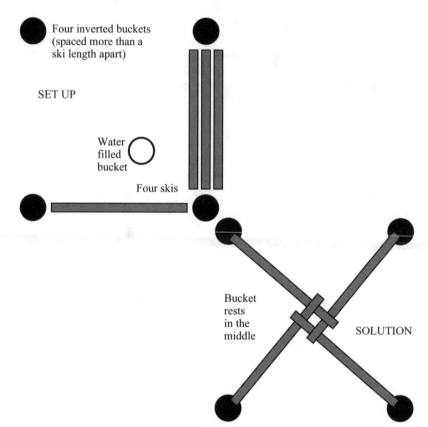

Four inverted buckets
(spaced more than a
ski length apart)

SET UP

Water
filled
bucket

Four skis

Bucket
rests
in the
middle

SOLUTION

One of the many reasons for developing teamwork is to enhance a corporation and elevate it to new levels of achievement. In this activity, we will need to prevent our corporation (water bucket) from sinking toward insolvency (staying on the ground) and raise it to higher accomplishments (support it above ground). One way to do this is by helping a corporation's people to create support from it's rock solid resources like information (stationary inverted buckets) and it's flexible resources like finances (movable skis). Unfortunately, an elevated corporation cannot rest solely on any single source of information (water bucket can't sit over any one inverted bucket) and finances must be kept away from potential insolvency (skis can't touch the ground). Any questions?

Action: Group attempts to suspend a bucket of water using two pairs of skis resting on four inverted buckets.

Intent: Problem solving, creativity, cooperation, communication, trust, and leadership.

Note: The original problem utilized 4 knives and 5 bottles (substitute popsicle sticks and foam cups when working indoors).

Equipment: Two pairs of skis (four skis of the same reasonable length) and five buckets (one filled with water).

Setup: Place the four empty buckets upside down in a square, as close as possible together, but just over one ski length apart (so one ski can't rest on two buckets). Put the water filled bucket and four skis inside this square.

Task: Suspend the water filled bucket (above ground level) using only the skis and without breaking any rules.

Constraints: Do not move any of the inverted empty buckets (which must remain more than a ski length apart). The skis may not touch the ground in any way. The water bucket may not be placed above or directly over any inverted bucket.

Safety: Watch out for heavy equipment (especially the water filled bucket) being dropped on people.

Facilitation: Once the group has solved this, challenge them to try it with one less skis and one less bucket, then again with all four skis, but only two buckets. Debrief for creative problem solving and sharing of ideas.

Variations: Aside from the variations listed above, try super sizing this with 55 gallon drums and wooden planks.

12   Life: A Balancing Act

PROPS: 2   **TIME:** 10-20   **ALIAS:** The Porcupine, BBA-102
MOVE: 0   **SIZE:** 10-20   **ORIGIN:** MIT Engineers, via K.R.

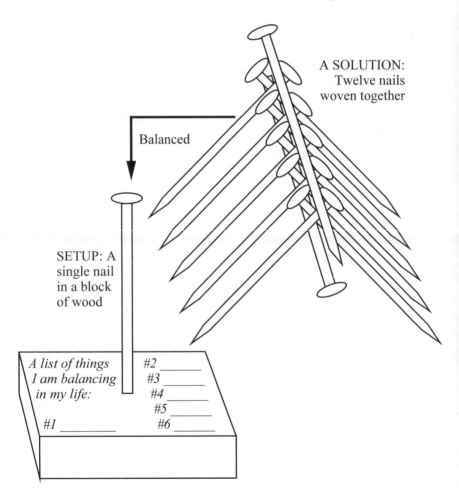

A SOLUTION:
Twelve nails
woven together

Balanced

SETUP: A
single nail
in a block
of wood

*A list of things
I am balancing
in my life:*

#1 _____
#2 _____
#3 _____
#4 _____
#5 _____
#6 _____

This activity is about balancing work and family.   Please make a list of twelve things you are balancing right now and write these on the block.... Now that you have your list, consider yourself (the center nail) linked to an organization (the block), with twelve things to balance (other nails) on your shoulders (atop the center nail).   Do this now (balance twelve nails atop the one) without any additional aid (no external support).   Any questions?

Action: Individuals attempt to weave 12 nails into some kind of design that can be balanced atop another nail.

Intent: Problem solving, creativity, sharing ideas, cooperation, and communication.

Note: This can be super-sized for big groups by making nails from PVC piping with flat caps or t-junctions.

Equipment: A pen, 13 common flat head nails (as long as possible) and a wood block (one set for each person).

Setup: Pound one nail about 20% of its length into the block of wood. Lay the other 12 nails beside the wood.

Task: To simultaneously balance a dozen nails atop the head of the thirteenth without breaking any of the rules.

Constraints: Nails cannot rest on the wood or anywhere else (nails must be free to fall off or stay on). No additional props (glue or magnetism) may be used. Nails cannot be deformed, bent or broken (use as they are).

Safety: Remind people that the nails will have sharp ends.

Facilitation: A solution comes from listing the attributes of common style nails (flat head). Discuss the role that attribute listing played in creative problem solving. Debrief whether ideas, failures and solutions were shared. Discuss the trials and tribulations of balancing life, paying particular attention to work and families or friends.

Variations: The nice thing about the super-sized version with pipe as described above, is that each person can have responsibility for one giant nail and can contribute equally to the final solution. Challenge the group to find an alternative solution to this problem (we've seen a half dozen others). How few or many nails can be balanced?

13   Office Wiring, etc.

PROPS: 0   **TIME:** 10-20   **ALIAS:** Assorted Puzzles, NEW
MOVE: 0   **SIZE:** 10-20   **ORIGIN:** Classics via S.P.

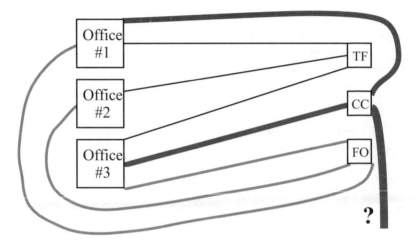

A PARTIAL SOLUTION

Junction Boxes and Wiring Types

TF=Telephone/Fax   ——————

CC=Coaxial Cable   ▬▬▬▬▬

FO=Fiber Optics   ——————

WIRING THE OFFICE -- You have three offices that need to be wired from three different junction boxes: telephone/fax; coaxial cable; and fiber optics. Unfortunately, magnetic interference from each type of wiring suppresses all three types of transmissions. Since shielded wiring is not available and because all wiring must remain grounded (can't go into the air to distribute its interference everywhere), trace the route that the three types of wires will take from their junction boxes to the offices without crossing one another. Any questions?

Action: Group sits down in a circle and discusses one or more of ten puzzles.

Intent: Problem Solving, creativity, and analytical thinking.

Note: Any puzzle will do for this sedentary activity. Ten examples of varying difficulty are provided here.

Equipment: None, but people may want to use pen and paper to figure out some of the puzzles. As the facilitator, decide in advance if this will be okay.

Setup: Simply present the puzzles below or any on the next four pages and let the group discuss these as necessary. If supplying them with diagrams (like the one below), omit the lines that make the answer easier.

Task: Answer the puzzles (the first one should be easier given the diagram above).

Constraints: None, other than those self imposed by the groups' collective thinking process.

Safety: No physical concerns, unless these become active experiences by adding props to make real puzzles.

Facilitation: Observe the group process and debrief around how well ideas were shared and what creative or analytical breakthroughs helped to solve the problem. Discuss teamwork in relation to these kind of problems.

Variations: The following four pages contain 9 more brain teasers. Many of these can be turned into experiential exercises through the use of props. Here is the solution to the puzzle opposite:

WIRING THE OFFICE -- This two dimensional problem can only be solved by thinking in three dimensions. While the last wire cannot leave the ground and hop over any of the other wires, it can go underground and arrive next to the last office. Instead of solving this on flat paper, try solving it in 3D on a donut.

9 Questions

POLE VAULT POLES & AIRLINE RESTRICTIONS -- *A person purchases a new pole vault pole that is almost 13 feet long and attempts to check it as luggage on board a domestic air flight. The airline has restrictions that they will carry nothing outside the maximum dimensions (12' long, 4' wide, and 3' thick) and so refuses to permit carriage. The owner quickly grabs a taxi to the nearest store and returns with the problem solved. Without cutting up the pole, bending it to fit, or changing its length, how was the crisis averted?*

THE ODDS OF AN EXECUTION -- *You are a political prisoner facing execution at the hands of an unusually playful executioner. The executioner gives you two boxes of poker chips: one contains 100 red chips and the other has 100 blue ones. The executioner, after becoming blindfolded, will pick one box and then pick one chip from that box. If a blue chip is chosen you will be set free; but if a red chip is selected, you will be put to death. You may rearrange the 200 chips among the two boxes anyway you like, but no box can be left empty and no chips may be hidden or changed. How do you rearrange them to maximize your odds of freedom?*

MARRIAGE VERSUS DEATH -- *Two young people are in love and wish to be married against the will of their evil guardians (who are only caring for the couple, while hoping someday to gain access to their inheritances). The guardians meet the couple on the beach of a neutral island between the two family's lands. After much discussion, they all agree to the luck of the draw deciding their fates. Two pebbles will be selected from a wide variety of beach stones and be placed in a bag. If the couple draw a white one they may be married, but if they draw a black one they will be killed (and the guardians will get their money). As the stones are gathered by a guardian, the couple notice that only two black stones and no white ones go in the bag! How do they avoid death and manage to get married, without angering or exposing any guardian as a liar or a cheat?*

WHAT COLOR IS YOUR HAT? -- *A professor wished to determine who was the smartest of his graduate students. He brought them into his office, blindfolded them, covered all the mirrors in the room, and sat them in chairs facing one another. He told them that he would put either a yellow or a green hat on their heads, but then placed green ones on the heads of all three students! He then told them to remove their blindfolds and to look at one another, but not their own heads. He asked, "Raise your hand if you see at least one green hat," to which all three raised a hand. Next, he said, "Stand up if you know the color of the hat on your head." After a lengthy pause, only one student stood up and correctly stated the color of her hat was green. How was this known?*

9 Answers

POLE VAULT POLES & AIRLINE RESTRICTIONS -- The pole will fit if placed diagonally in a box that meets the maximum size restrictions of the airlines. Use the Pythagorean Theorem for right angled triangles: the square of the hypotenuse is equal to the sum of the squares of both sides. Therefore, the base of the box will have a 5' diagonal ($3^2 + 4^2 = 9 + 16 = 25 = 5^2$) and the internal diagonal will be 13' ($5^2 + 12^2 = 25 + 144 = 169 = 13^2$).

THE ODDS OF AN EXECUTION -- If you place 199 chips in one box and leave a single blue chip in the other box, then the odds of getting set free climb toward 75%. First, the executioner has a 50% chance of picking the box with the single blue chip of freedom. However, if the box with 199 chips is chosen, then there is a further 25% chance of picking one of the 99 blue chips (50% of the other 50%) and not one of the 100 red ones. Total odds are almost 75%.

MARRIAGE VERSUS DEATH -- Draw a stone, look at it in a way no one else can see, and then throw it as far away as possible (into the ocean or across the beach of a million similar stones) and rejoice for you are to be wed! Disbelief? Simply ask the guardians to check the color of the stone left in the bag. If it is black (death) you must have thrown away the white (marriage) stone out of excitement.

WHAT COLOR IS YOUR HAT? -- Three students (A B C) all have green hats on their heads. Student A's logic goes like this. I saw B and C raise a hand indicating they saw at least one green hat, but they could have seen each others' green hats. Therefore, my hat could be green or yellow. Assuming my hat is green doesn't get me any new information, so I'll assume (for now) that my hat is yellow. Now I wonder what B and C would have thought when we all raised our hands and they saw me wearing a (supposedly) yellow hat? If my hat really was yellow, then B would have assumed that C was raising a hand for a green hat on B's head, but B didn't realize this, since B didn't stand up. Similarly, if my hat really was yellow, then C would have assumed that B was raising a hand for a green hat on C's head, but C didn't realize this either, since C didn't stand up. Therefore, I can't have a yellow hat on my head. It must be green! We're all slow to stand up, because all our hats are green.

HOW MANY CUTS & SEGMENTS? -- *A woman is late to pay back a loan and makes a unfortunate agreement with her loan shark. For every day late, she will owe further compounded interest on the loan, but must provide suitable collateral. She offers her gold necklace as collateral, but refuses to give up the entire necklace. They agree that she will surrender one of the links per day until the end of the month (the necklace has 31 links). By month's end, she will have paid the loan plus interest or she will lose the entire necklace. Both parties agree that 30 cuts of the necklace into 31 single segments will be costly to disassemble and extremely expensive to reassemble. They agree that a minimum number of cuts will be made to keep the necklace in as few segments as possible and that the loan shark will exchange shorter segments for longer ones as necessary. What is the optimal arrangement of the situation: how many cuts, how many segments, and how many links for each segment?*

THE MINER'S SCALES -- *A miner has a 40 pound stone that is used to weigh ore on a balance scale. A friend borrows the stone to weigh ore from a neighboring claim and, while caring for the stone, it gets dropped and broken into 4 pieces. Each piece is a different size and weight, but all weights are exact to the nearest precise pound! The miner is not disappointed, because the new weights permit ore to be weighed pound by pound from 1 to 40 pounds. What are the four stone's weights?*

15 SECOND FUSE -- *You have two fuses of the type that are ignited by open flame and that burn with sparks and plenty of smoke. These fuses burn continuously for 60 seconds each. While the duration is precise, the rate of burn is not steady. Each fuse could simmer for seconds and then advance rapidly only to pause again. So, you cannot create shorter fuses by simply cutting a sixty second fuse in half to make two 30 second fuses. How would you measure a 15 second period of time, given that you only have the fuses and no watch?*

OPTIONS & CONSULTANTS -- *You have two choices: option A and option B. One gives absolute success, while the other leads to certain failure, but you do not know which is which. Two consultants know the answers: Dr. X and Dr. Y. However, one is a constant liar, while the other is always truthful, but again, you don't know which is which. You can ask one question, of one consultant, once only before having to choose your best option. What is your question, who do you ask, and what do you do with the answer you receive?*

LIGHT SWITCHES -- *You have three light switches (all set in the off position) connected to a lone light bulb (also turned off) placed in a distant room. Only one of the switches works (the other two are dead). You will only be permitted to visit this room ONCE. After your visit, you must decide which of the*   CONT.—>

HOW MANY CUTS & SEGMENTS? -- Four cuts, into five segments, with 1, 2, 4, 8 & 16 links respectively (1=1, 2=2, 3=1+2, 4=4, 5=4+1, 6=4+2, 7=4+2+1, 8=8, 9=8+1, 10=8+2, 11=8+2+1, 12=8+4, 13=8+4+1, 14=8+4+2, 15=8+4+2+1, 16=16, 17=16+1, 18=16+2, 19=16+2+1, 20=16+4, 21=16+4+1, 22=16+4+2, 23=16+4+2+1, 24=16+8, 25=16+8+1, 26=16+8+2, 27=16+8+2+1, 28=16+8+4, 29=16+8+4+1, 30=16+8+4+2, and 31=16+8+4+2+1).

THE MINER'S SCALES -- The four stones weigh 1, 3, 9 & 27 pounds respectively (1=1, 2=3-1, 3=3, 4=3+1, 5=9-3-1, 6=9-3, 7=9-3+1), 8=9-1, 9=9, 10=9+1, 11=9+3-1, 12=9+3, 13=9+3+1, 14=27-9-3-1, 15=27-9-3, 16=27-9-3+1, 17=27-9-1, 18=27-9, 19=27-9+1, 20=27-9+3-1, 21=27-9+3, 22=27-9+3+1, 23=27-3-1, 24=27-3, 25=27-3+1, 26=27-1, 27=27, 28=27+1, 29=27+3-1, 30=27+3, 31=27+3+1, 32=27+9-3-1, 33=27+9-3, 34=27+9-3+1, 35=27+9-1, 36=27+9, 37=27+9+1, 38=27+9+3-1, 39=27+9+3, and 40=27+9+3+1).

15 SECOND FUSE -- Simultaneously light both ends of one fuse AND one end of the other fuse (do this by placing all three ends in a bundle and lighting them together, but hold onto the fourth end). The first 60 second fuse will now burn from both ends in exactly 30 seconds. At the time when this happens, the second fuse will have 30 seconds left. At this very moment, light the fourth end and the remaining fuse will burn for 15 seconds.

OPTIONS & CONSULTANTS -- Since you do not know which option leads to success or failure, and you do not know which consultant tells the truth or lies, you will need to involve at least three of these items in your question. Ask any consultant which option the other consultant will identify as the successful one and then choose the opposite option! By cross referencing the two consultants, you are certain that the answer you receive will definitely be a lie. Since you are sure to get the wrong answer, simply reverse it and pick the opposite option.

LIGHT SWITCHES -- Turn two switches on and wait five minutes before turning one of these two off again. When you check the light, examine it for temperature as well. If the light is on, then the live switch is the one you left on; and if the light is off and cold, then the live switch is the one you left off; but if the light is off and warm, then the live switch is the one you originally turned on and then turned off again after five minutes.

---

switches is the live one. Before your visit, you may arrange the switches anyway you like, but may not open the switch box, may not peek into the room through windows, doors or walls, and may not make similar bypasses. What do you do?

14   **Reorganizing Inventory**

PROPS: 1   **TIME:** 10-20   **ALIAS:** Towers of Hanoi, NEW
MOVE: 0   **SIZE:** 5-10   **ORIGIN:** Classic via S.P.

SETUP

ACTION: The first 6 moves of a 31 move solution

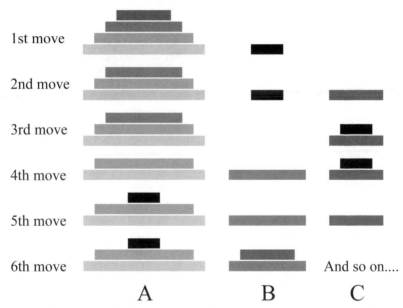

1st move

2nd move

3rd move

4th move

5th move

6th move   And so on....

A   B   C

Our warehouse stocks five closely related items: staples, paper clips, tape, index cards, and paper sheets. These are stored in different containers (each one indicated by a colored ring). Unfortunately, we have to move warehouses (spaces) and your task is to develop a system for reorganizing the inventory according to a series of required procedures. First, to avoid crushing, no larger container can sit atop a smaller one. Second, only one container can be moved at a time. Third, containers may only be moved into warehouses and may not be placed anywhere else. When finished, please report the minimum number of moves for your system. Any questions?

Action: The group attempts to discover the minimum number of moves needed to rearrange a tower of rings.

Intent: Problem solving, communication, cooperation, trust, analytical thinking, and planning.

Note: This activity can be supersized with lighter inner tubes or heavier truck tires placed over 3' high posts anchored in the ground.

Equipment: A stack of 5 Rocker Rings (a preschool play toy) and a suitable table space (marked with 3 spaces).

Setup: Place the stack of rings in one of 3 open spaces, perhaps in a line (as shown in the diagram) or in a triangular or L-shaped arrangement.

Task: To disassemble the rings of a tower on one space and reassemble them as a tower again on another space in a minimum number of moves.

Constraints: No big rings atop small ones. No rings anywhere other than in the spaces. Move one ring at a time.

Safety: No physical concerns (unless working with heavy tires or inner tubes in a super-sized version).

Facilitation: The minimum number of moves varies with the number of rings (2 rings = 3 moves, 3 rings = 7 moves, 4 rings = 15 moves, 5 rings = 31 moves, 6 rings = 63 moves, 7 rings = 127 moves, and 8 rings = 255 moves). Discuss communication, sharing of ideas, leadership, analytical thinking, and problem solving. Ask groups to demonstrate their solutions: do they remember it or write it down? Can everyone perform it accurately?

Variations: Break larger groups into smaller ones and let them use phones, radios, and/or walkie talkies to communicate. Examine how they share information.

15 Passwords & Combinations

PROPS: 1   **TIME:** 20-30   **ALIAS:** Neat Puzzle, FSI-36
MOVE: 1   **SIZE:** 9-25   **ORIGIN:** David Wheatley, S.P.

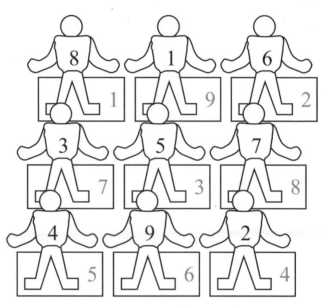

ACTION: Shows first half (magic square) completed

0 = numbers assigned to people

0 = numbers hidden under spaces

You have 10 minutes to complete each of two tasks to open a time lock: submit a computerized password and then dial a bank vault combination. Submit the password by arranging yourselves on the nine bank vault tumblers (spaces) so that the sum of your numbers are the same for all 3 rows, 3 columns, and 2 diagonals (this is a magic square). You get one attempt to be correct, or the system locks for 24 hours. Any questions? Okay, step on in the next 10 minutes.... Now that you have computer access by submitting the correct password, dial the combination by aligning your numbers with those in the tumblers (hidden beneath each space). Tumblers can only hold one number at a time (one person per space). Exchange numbers simultaneously only between adjacent tumblers (people can swap horizontal or vertical spaces, but not diagonal ones). Examine a tumbler (look for the hidden number under only one space) between each exchange (after making one swap). You have 10 minutes.

Action: Group members move around to position themselves on spaces to solve arithmetic problems.

Intent: Analytical thinking, problem solving, communication, and cooperation.

Note: This requires a minimum of nine people (any more than nine can observe and participate from the side).

Equipment: Nine spaces (carpet squares or paper sheets) for nine people. More spaces for the other variations.

Setup: Place the nine spaces on the floor in a 3 by 3 square. Randomly place or write hidden numbers 1 through 9 beneath the nine spaces. Assemble nine people (others observing) and assign them the numbers 1 through 9.

Task: To solve a magic square and to find their proper places by matching their numbers to each space's number.

Constraints: Ten minute time limits and only one magic square try. Remain on your space (no space sharing), switch at same time with adjacent people (no diagonal switches), and look under one space between each switch.

Safety: If people look like they will lose their balance from passing carefully, then permit temporary step offs.

Facilitation: Check that all eight magic square sums total to 15. Debrief for problem solving and cooperation.

Variations: Use larger squares for bigger groups: a more difficult 4 by 4 square or an extremely tough 5 by 5. Here are some solutions.

MAGIC SQUARE
SOLUTIONS

8	1	6
3	5	7
4	9	2

16	3	2	13
5	10	11	8
9	6	7	12
4	15	14	1

17	24	1	8	15
23	5	7	14	16
4	6	13	20	22
10	12	19	21	3
11	18	25	2	9

3 by 3 square   4 by 4 square   5 by 5 square
(eight sums = 15)   (ten sums = 34)   (twelve sums = 65)

16 Raising Group Performance

PROPS: 1   **TIME:** 10-30   **ALIAS:** Washtub Willies, NEW
MOVE: 3   **SIZE:** 2-20   **ORIGIN:** Sam Sikes

ACTION: Lifting the
tub with one shoe
on and one shoe off

This activity is about what each of you do together to raise your team performance. Here we have a representation of your team (washtub) and the sustaining contributions each of you brings to the team (your feet). As you place your supporting assistance against the team (put your feet against the washtub), I'd like each person to pledge something that you will offer the team to ensure its future improvement and success.... Thank you for making those commitments. Now that your promises are supporting the team, let's raise its performance to new heights (lift the washtub a few feet off the ground without using your hands).... Great, now as you support your team with your contributions (keep washtub raised off the ground), we know that sometimes we lose commitment (so please take off one shoe to represent this).... Good, we know that commitment can also be reinforced by one's co-workers (so please help each other to put the shoe back on before you lower the washtub).

Action: A sitting group uses their feet to raise a washtub full of water off the ground without spilling any of its contents.

Intent: Coordinated movement, cooperation, communication, trust, problem solving, and commitment.

Note: If concerned about spilling water indoors, simply fill the washtub with dried beans or similar materials.

Equipment: A metal washtub that is almost full of water (or suitable substitute).

Setup: Put the almost filled washtub on the ground and ask the group to face the tub and sit in a circle around it.

Task: To raise the tub, remove one shoe each, and put the shoe back on with the help of others, and then lower the washtub back down.

Constraints: Use your feet (no hands) on the tub. Pledge a commitment prior to fully engaging in the activity.

Safety: Obviously take care to spot and to prevent the washtub or its contents from getting dropped on anyone.

Facilitation: Discuss the interdependence of both task and relationship factors of team performance. Debrief for commitment, cooperation, and communication. Did folks meet their commitments as they initially promised?

Variations: Try taking off both shoes, with some people blindfolded and others muted, or everyone non-verbal.

17   Serving Customers

PROPS: 2 **TIME:** 10-20 **ALIAS:** Balloon Foosball, EM-12
MOVE: 2 **SIZE:** 10-100 **ORIGIN:** Sam Sikes & Karl Rohnke

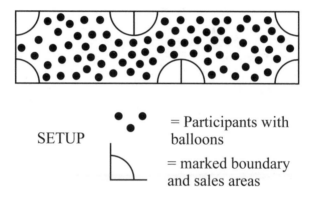

SETUP

• •
•

= Participants with balloons

= marked boundary and sales areas

You are a floor walker in one of our stores. Each of you has the initial accountability for one customer (indicate the balloons) who is asking for help in finding a specific shopping sales area (marked off areas). We have several kinds of customers seeking pharmacy (white), fashions (orange), hardware (blue), electronics (red), housewares (green), gardening (yellow), toys (purple), etc. Since we are interested in seeing that each individual is cared for in a manner consistent with our mission, you will be expected to help each one toward their sales area via the next floor walker along the way. As this happens, you may find yourself juggling several customers at a time, simply do your best to pass them on to another floor walker. If customers should NOT receive the care they require (balloons drop to the ground), then we would expect anyone who finds lost customers to help them on their way again (pick up the balloons and rejuggle them). If any customers should leave the store (balloons fall outside the boundary markers), then they are obviously taking their business elsewhere and we will consider that a lost sale (you may not leave the area at any time to retrieve or transport balloons). Since floor walkers are not often able to communicate easily, we will continue the activity nonverbally. Any questions before we start? GO!

Action: A large group of people attempt to juggle colored balloons into designated color-coded sales areas.

Intent: Community building, sense of immediate success and accomplishment.

Note: This activity may be competitive at the start. Simply go with the group atmosphere and then adapt.

Equipment: At least one large balloon per person (multiple colors), rope or tape to mark boundaries and areas.

Setup: In a large room or outside field (free of wind), mark boundaries and sales areas (perhaps corners or sides of the field). Assign colors to each sales area. Give everyone a balloon, ask them to inflate it and tie off the neck. Have them non-verbally practice juggling all the balloons in the air without dropping them. Organize people into teams or one large community depending on whether an emphasis on competition or cooperation is desired.

Task: To get all the balloons into the same colored and marked areas without losing any of them out-of-bounds.

Constraints: Conduct the activity non-verbally. People are free to move (this was purposefully not mentioned).

Safety: Stretch, spread out, and emphasize no contact to avoid bumping or hitting one another with flailing arms.

Facilitation: If organized into teams, announcements like "First team to collect all of one's customers wins" can add to the competition factor and may sometimes result in some folks stealing customers as they pass by (thus preventing sales from being made elsewhere). Sometimes the juggling practice is enough to set a precedent, but decide whether holding and transporting balloons (this is the most effective way of caring) will be permitted. If the organization is attempting to be collaborative, then competition (and the behaviors that arise from this) will obviously diminish the company's unity: one team may win, but the majority of other teams will lose for a net organizational loss. Balloons that get stepped on, and perhaps pop loudly, make for interesting discussions about caring.

Variations: Allow people or groups to choose the colors for sales areas. Once balloons have been moved into these sales areas, designate people to collect the balloons in large clear plastic bags. Have people sit or stand still or try the activity verbally.

18   Hiring Staff to Fit the Job

PROPS: 2   **TIME:** 10-20   **ALIAS:** Balloon in a Glass, NEW
MOVE: 0   **SIZE:** 2-100   **ORIGIN:** Jim Willis

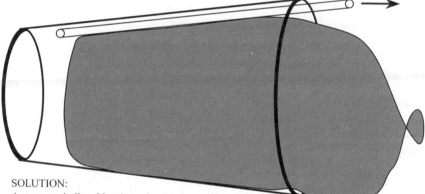

SOLUTION:
A straw or similar object is used to let air escape

Your partnership has an employment opportunity (tumbler) and a job applicant (balloon). Please fill this position (put the balloon in the tumbler) and make sure the fit is perfect (use all the balloon). If person or position don't fit perfectly (balloon sticks out), further training is needed (try again). Any questions?

Action: Pairs of people attempt to insert a balloon filled with water into a tumbler without bursting the balloon.

Intent: Identifying the crux of a problem, sharing ideas, cooperation, and communication.

Note: Tumblers narrowing toward their base work better than cylindrical ones. Bavarian beer glasses work best.

Equipment: Tumblers and balloons filled with a tumbler's worth of water. Straws are hidden elsewhere.

Setup: Give a balloon filled with water and a tumbler to each partnership (or give one a tumbler and the other a balloon).

Task: To get a balloon filled with water inside a tumbler without any of the balloon sticking out of the tumbler.

Constraints: Other props may be used to help you, but the balloon may not be burst or damaged in any way.

Safety: Get ready for some water spills and possibly slippery floors. Have spare balloon filled with water available. Discourage the use of thin sided tumblers and sharp or hard objects to prod the balloon into place.

Facilitation: The solution lies in identifying the crux as getting air out of the tumbler rather than getting water in. Once this is known, people usually find straws or strawlike objects that permit the air to escape as the balloon is pressed into the glass. Debrief for problem solving and how identifying the crux can make all the difference. How widely were good ideas shared? Once people solved the problem, did they keep the answers to themselves?

Variations: To make this easier, place strawlike objects (pens with removable centers or straws) in plain view.

19 Reorganizing the Hierarchy

PROPS: 1   **TIME:** 20-30   **ALIAS:** Continuous Circle, SB-131
MOVE: 1   **SIZE:** 2-20   **ORIGIN:** Classic

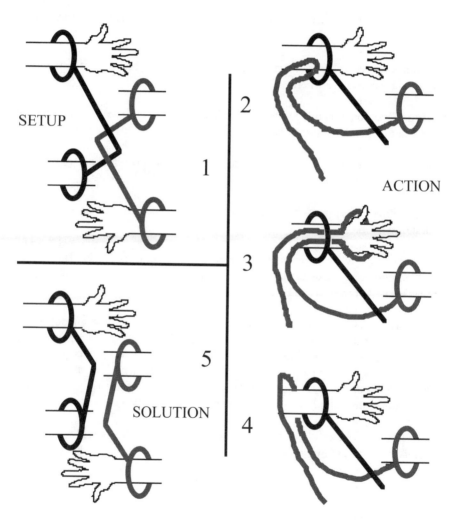

SETUP

1

2

ACTION

3

5

SOLUTION

4

This arrangement represents your normal group's accountability. Before we can reorganize it, you need to dissolve these accountable linkages (become unconnected) without removing your own responsibilities (can't take off loops, cut the cords, or untie knots). Any questions?

Action: People connected by several intertwined handcuffed wrist loop cords attempt to disconnect themselves.

Intent: Problem solving, sharing ideas, cooperation and communication.

Note: This can be attempted by one person using their own wrists and a second set of ankle cuffs on their feet.

Equipment: One 6' length of cord for each person. If you have variable lengths, the longest ones should be given to the bosses.

Setup: Tie loops in both ends of each piece of cord with a simple overhand knot. Ask each person to take a length of cord and place the loops over each wrist, so the result is a soft pair of handcuffs. Next, take the group and link them according to their natural hierarchy. For example, the director is connected to 3 managers who report to that director and each manager is connected to 5 or 6 supervisors who report to that manager (one person might get linked to 2 or more other people, if they have multiple reporting relationships). Create these linkages by removing one wrist loop from a superordinate and passing it through all the other handcuffs of the subordinates before reattaching that loop to the boss' wrist again. The result should be a series of tangles.

Task: To get untangled from one another's handcuffing wrist loops without breaking any of the rules.

Constraints: While knots may be loosened for comfort (purposefully not mentioned because it leads to the solution), knots must not be undone. Do not cut the ropes or remove the loops from any wrists.

Safety: People will initially attempt to climb over one another and/or contort their bodies to get out of the bind. Permit any motions that do not cause pain or injury, and be prepared to spot people who go off the ground.

Facilitation: Initially, this seems impossible, so continue to share that a solution exists. One solution is to pass a bight (looped bit) of the cord through a wrist loop of the neighbor (with the curved piece of the bight going toward their finger tips) and then pass that bight over their hand and then pull it back through the wrist loop once again. Debrief for how the solution was first achieved and whether it was shared with others once it was found.

Variations: To make this easier, place people in pairs, have them try with their partners, and then see if the solution is shared or kept secret from others.

20   Supporting your Leader

PROPS: 1   **TIME:** 20-30   **ALIAS:** Duct Tape, FSII-38
MOVE: 1   **SIZE:** 10-30   **ORIGIN:** Karl Rohnke, Simon Priest

ONE
SOLUTION

In this activity, you'll be supporting your leader as s/he takes a risk. Your basic tools of support are the behaviors you bring to encourage, comfort, strengthen, and sustain others in times of duress and anxiety. In fact, I'd like each of you to tear off a short piece of tape and (using this marker) write the behavior which you bring to support this leader.... Now, as you offer your contribution (stick your piece of tape) to your leader, tell us a little about it.... Lastly, using all the contributions you have (remaining tape) support your leader without external aid (no chair) for 15 seconds. You have 5 minutes to plan and 10 minutes to offer help (apply tape). Any questions?

Action: The group secures one member (usually their designated leader) to a wall using a roll of duct tape.

Intent: Planning, deinhibitization, cooperation, communication, trust, support.

Note: The leader must be suitably clothed for this activity to work properly (emphasize challenge by choice).

Equipment: A thick felt tipped marker, a chair and a single 60' roll of the best duct tape available.

Setup: Find an appropriate wall with a surface that adheres to duct tape and where the paint doesn't come loose when a test strip is ripped off. Bring the group to the wall and give them a single roll of tape. Position a chair beside the wall and invite the well-clothed leader to stand on the chair and lean back against or face the wall.

Task: Secure a team leader to the wall so that s/he will stay suspended for 15 seconds once the chair is removed.

Constraints: Tape must be applied flat to the wall and may not go around corners or over the top. You have 15 minutes to discuss and actually tape the leader in place. After this total 15 minutes, the chair will be removed.

Safety: If a leader is not committed to this, allow him/her to substitute someone else. Spot the leader as necessary while standing on the chair and when the chair gets removed. Avoid taping over hair or skin, and especially the face, neck or very hairy skin. Encourage the leader to wear lots of clothing in advance.

Facilitation: An organized group that thinks about the physics of tape application will achieve almost 100% success in this activity. A group that overplans or does no planning at all is predictably in trouble. Debrief the value of planning versus paralysis by analysis. Here are some technical rules of tape application not to be shared with the group: V-shapes for vectors hold tape better than horizontal pieces, long pieces hold better than short, and tape applied over tape is tape wasted. Do not discuss the physics, but rather concentrate on the process of support.

Variations: Ordinarily, 3 people can be successfully suspended with a roll of duct tape, so choose a few leaders. Challenge high performing teams to maximize the number of people suspended and the time they are supported or to achieve maximum support and suspension with a minimum amount of tape and time.

21   **Product Packaging**

PROPS: 2   **TIME:** 30-60   **ALIAS:** Egg Drop, CC-85
MOVE: 1   **SIZE:**   3-10   **ORIGIN:** Classic

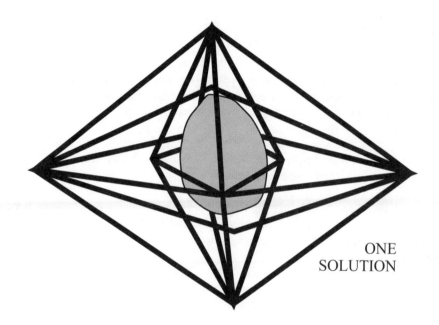

ONE
SOLUTION

Your company has been asked to design a complete packaging system for a new fragile product (hold up an egg). The packaging must be created from these two materials (straws and tape) that are the only ones resistant to the adverse influences of the product (all other resources are unavailable for use). Once your designs are finished, we will test them with a series of drops from increasing heights (indicate drop area). Designs may not be altered in any manner once the testing begins. The group with the system that withstands multiple drops from increasing heights without any damage of the product (the last egg to break), wins the contract for mass production of that packaging system. Any questions?... Extra points will be awarded for dramatic presentations and enlightened explanations of each system. You have 30 minutes to plan and construct your systems. GO!

Action: Group builds a structure out of straws and tape to protect raw eggs from breaking when dropped from a specified height.

Intent: Planning, problem solving, idea sharing, competition, cooperation, and communication.

Note: Substitute hard boiled eggs for raw ones to avoid the possibility of having to clean up a real mess.

Equipment: One egg, 24 rigid drinking straws, and 4' of masking tape per group. A ladder and plastic tarp.

Setup: Find a position of height (use a ladder if necessary) with a hard landing surface (spread a plastic tarp as needed). Break into several smaller groups of 3 - 5 people and distribute materials (raw egg, straws and tape).

Task: To protect a raw egg from breaking when dropped from increasing heights by building protective systems.

Constraints: Use only the materials provided (straws and tape). Designs may not be changed between drops.

Safety: If a ladder is used, have someone hold it firmly, and spot anyone who climbs up the ladder.

Facilitation: The product of protecting the egg is not as important here as the process of sharing ideas among groups in the same company to get the best overall design. Debrief around this concept and whether the groups work together or compete. Start with low heights of a few feet and work up from there. Some designs have worked well from a height of several stories. If all designs fail at the same height, judge them with extra criteria.

Variations: Restrict planning and construction times. Add nonverbal constraints. Permit more tries and an opportunity for group representatives to meet and compare learning. Place greater emphasis on the presentation of an appropriate commercial jargon, a catchy jingle or song, and a flashy visual presentation of the device itself.

22   Reaching the Sales Quota

PROPS: 1   **TIME:** 20-30   **ALIAS:** Paper Drop, QS-179
MOVE: 1   **SIZE:** 3-20   **ORIGIN:** Karl Rohnke, Sam Sikes

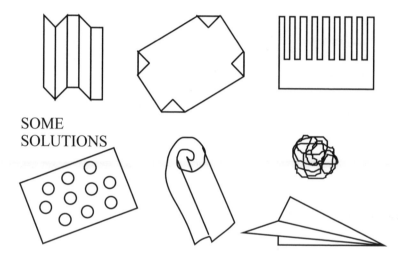

SOME
SOLUTIONS

Your groups are pitching sales (dropping paper) to customers (targets) from your offices (the balcony). For every customer contacted (show paper hitting target), you will receive $10,000 in future considerations; and for every customer sold (show paper staying on target), you will receive $50,000. Today's quota is $200,000 for 20 pitches (therefore, you need to land on three targets and hit five, or a similar combination). Any reasonable type of sales pitch is permissible (modify paper as you like, but don't use other resources) and you must decide how to make your best 20 sales pitches. Lastly, you may leave bits out of a sales pitch (tear off corners), but these leftover bits cannot be pitched separately (can't drop the corners). Unfortunately, you can't leave your office and you must not add anything to your sales pitch (no moisture or weights). Any questions?

Action: Small groups drop various modified sheets of paper in order to hit and/or land on targets.

Intent: Planning, problem solving, idea sharing, competition, cooperation, and communication.

Note: This can consume lots of paper. To save a tree, consider using scrap paper already bound for recycling.

Equipment: Twenty sheets of paper per group and something to mark target areas (hula hoops or masking tape).

Setup: Find a place from where objects can be dropped safely (like a balcony) and lay out the targets below. Break the larger group into several smaller ones and give 20 sheets of paper to each group (use unique colors for each group).

Task: To drop sheets of paper to hit or land on targets, and to be allotted money on the basis of drop accuracy.

Constraints: You may tear, fold, or crumple any single sheet of paper, but sheets may not be combined. You may not add anything to the sheets (no moisture or weights). Anything subtracted from a sheet of paper must be kept in hand or remain attached to that dropped sheet. You must remain on the balcony when dropping sheets.

Safety: Discourage leaning over the edge of the balcony in an attempt to achieve added accuracy.

Facilitation: If the group runs out of paper before their daily quota has been met, feel free to creatively negotiate with them for additional sheets. If one group makes their quota, do they share leftover paper with others? Do the groups compete for the same customers or do they combine their quotas and work together to make the total? Be prepared to give some money for close calls ($5,000 for paper that passes nearby or falls close to targets). If the group comes up with unique solutions, like turning their sheet into a long thin streamer that lands on two targets at the same time, give double credit. If a drop hits two targets and lands on a third, give credit for all three.

Variations: Place an X on the ground and give points for proximity. Request an actual sales pitch (containing a product name, logo, catchy jingle or song, price, and flashy visual dramatization) from each group before a drop.

23   **Partners for Work**

PROPS: 1 **TIME:** 10-20 **ALIAS:** Paired Trust Walk, IG-41
MOVE: 2 **SIZE:** 2-20 **ORIGIN:** Classic

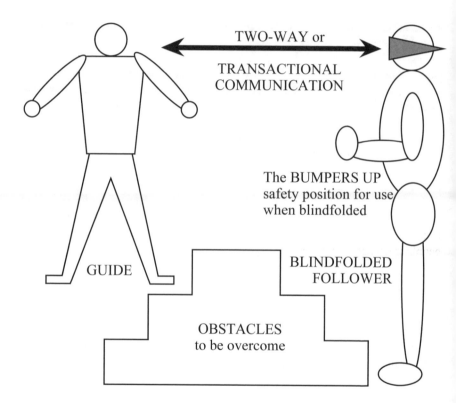

TWO-WAY or
TRANSACTIONAL
COMMUNICATION

The BUMPERS UP
safety position for use
when blindfolded

GUIDE

BLINDFOLDED
FOLLOWER

OBSTACLES
to be overcome

You are a rookie to the organization and this prevents you from seeing the pitfalls of the job (please put on your blindfold). Your partner is a veteran who knows how to avoid these pitfalls from experience, but does not know you well enough to help you fully (cannot touch you, but may speak to you). With the limited aid of your partner, find your way through the pitfalls of the first week at work (from start to finish through the obstacle area). Any questions?

Action: A blindfolded person travels through obstacles following the noncontact and verbal guidance of a partner.

Intent: Trust, two-way communication, risk taking, and support.

Note: Utilize simple obstacles and avoid placing people above the ground (blindfolded people are often anxious). Walking through shrubs, ducking under limbs, passing by running water, or going downhill are effective obstacles.

Equipment: A blindfold for each person. An area with natural obstacles (or obstacles that can be added in).

Setup: Walk though the obstacle area and be sure it is free of real dangers before choosing to use it. Assemble the group by the obstacle area. Have people pick partners and ask the pair to decide who will be blindfolded first.

Task: To walk through an obstacle area following the verbal directions of a partner who walks with you.

Constraints: You may speak with your partner, but may not touch one another. Roles will be reversed for a second attempt.

Safety: Remove and/or avoid dangerous obstacles. Encourage the blindfolded people to keep their bumpers up. If people are uncomfortable wearing a blindfold, ask them to remove it and be observers for rest of the activity.

Facilitation: Discuss issues related to partnership trust and communication, and then repeat with roles reversed.

Variations: Activity #37 is a suitable indoor alternative, but requires a large number of props.

24 Travelling in Foreign Lands

PROPS: 1 **TIME:** 20-40 **ALIAS:** Group Sherpa Walk, SB-89
MOVE: 2 **SIZE:** 5-20 **ORIGIN:** Outward Bound

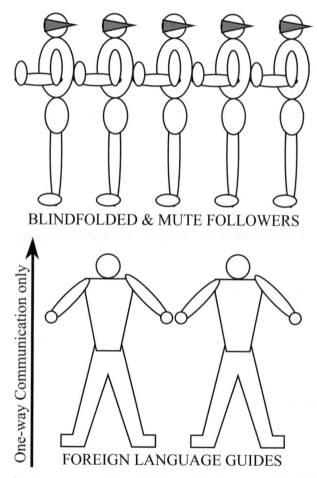

BLINDFOLDED & MUTE FOLLOWERS

One-way Communication only

FOREIGN LANGUAGE GUIDES

You are in a foreign country and are oblivious to local customs (blindfolded). Your guides do not speak your language and their culture prevents them from making physical contact with you (they cannot use words or touch you). Your guides do not understand English, so you have no need to speak to them (encourage the blindfolded folks to be mute as well). Your challenge is to overcome a series of obstacles as you travel through their business world (obstacle area). Any questions? Your guides will be with you shortly....

Action: A blindfolded group travels through obstacles following two guides who communicate without words.

Intent: Trust, one-way communication, and leadership.

Note: Utilize simple obstacles and avoid placing people above the ground (blindfolded people are often anxious). Walking through shrubs, ducking under limbs, passing by running water, or going downhill are effective obstacles.

Equipment: A blindfold for each person. An area with natural obstacles (or obstacles that can be added in).

Setup: Walk though the obstacle area and be sure it is free of real dangers before choosing to use it. Assemble the group by the obstacle area. Let the group choose two guides and ask all but the guides to put on blindfolds.

Task: For the sightless group to travel from start to finish through a series of obstacles with the aid of guides.

Constraints: While blind, the group must not speak and should maintain contact with one another. Guides must not touch the group in any manner, and may make any sound they wish, but may not use words to communicate.

Safety: Remove and/or avoid dangerous obstacles. Encourage the blindfolded people to keep their bumpers up. If people are uncomfortable wearing a blindfold, ask them to remove it and be observers for rest of the activity. If a path through the obstacles is not immediately obvious, walk ahead of the guides and show them the way to go. Let the group know that you will be silent, but present and will remain vigilant throughout the activity.

Facilitation: The guides typically figure out a communication system between themselves (whistles, claps, etc.) and then attempt to interpret this to the first person in the group. This first person then translates to the rest of the group through touch (remind the group not to talk at this point). Debrief for language and communication issues.

Variations: Permit the group to speak amongst themselves for greater ease and prevent them from touching each other to increase difficulty. Consider using multiple guides for larger groups. Use one guide for smaller groups.

25   Sharing a Common Vision

PROPS: 1   **TIME:** 10-30   **ALIAS:** Sheep Herding, GWA-39
MOVE: 2   **SIZE:** 5-20   **ORIGIN:** British Facilitators via S.P.

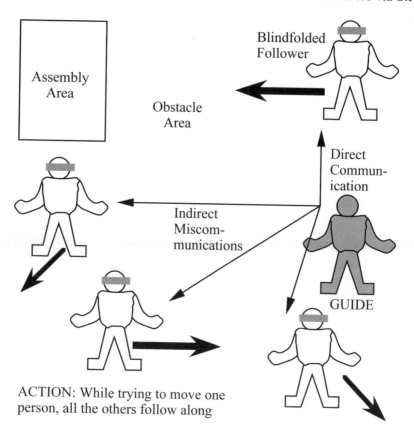

Assembly
Area

Blindfolded
Follower

Obstacle
Area

Direct
Commun-
ication

Indirect
Miscom-
munications

GUIDE

ACTION: While trying to move one
person, all the others follow along

In this activity, the organizational vision will be shared with your guide (who cannot move). Your guide has the job of getting everyone to come to a common understanding of that vision (reach an assembly area) before the deadline expires (20 minutes). Most of you have not heard or seen the vision (and so are blindfolded) and are beginning from an unorganized perspective (spread widely throughout this obstacle area). You will need to rely upon accurate communication from your guide in order to obtain the vision. Any questions?... Okay, you only have 5 minutes to plan! After that, you'll be blindfolded and dispersed, and your guide will receive the vision (take people to separate locations in the obstacle area, spin them around, and tell the guide where to gather them).

Action: A stationary guide gathers a dispersed blindfolded group and then herds them into an assembly area.

Intent: Trust, one-way and possibly two-way communication, and leadership.

Note: Utilize simple obstacles and avoid placing people above the ground (blindfolded people are often anxious). Due to the concern that one person may be trying to direct many others, use very few and very safe obstacles.

Equipment: A blindfold for each person. An area with natural obstacles (or obstacles that can be added in).

Setup: Walk though the obstacle area and be sure it is free of real dangers before choosing to use it. Assemble the group by the obstacle area. Let the group select one guide and ask all except that guide to put on a blindfold.

Task: To get a blindfolded group to gather in the same location after they start well dispersed within a large area.

Constraints: Planning time is 5 minutes only. Blindfolded folks are randomly distributed around the obstacle area (and turned about in circles a few times). The guide cannot move, but knows the assembly area location.

Safety: Remove and/or avoid dangerous obstacles. Encourage the blindfolded people to keep their bumpers up. If people are uncomfortable wearing a blindfold, ask them to remove it and be observers for rest of the activity. Some groups gather together and then herd as a group; while others herd as individuals before gathering together. Either way, be prepared to spot several people moving simultaneously within and outside the obstacle area.

Facilitation: During the brief planning session, if the group has not found a way to number off in advance to determine who will take turns receiving communication, then everyone begins moving in all directions once the guide begins talking. Functional groups will also include a feedback mechanism (like raising a hand) to indicate they know who is meant to receive communication. Debrief for miscommunications and leadership issues.

Variations: For less challenge, permit the blindfolded people to speak. For greater challenge, ask the guide to remain mute and use other sounds to communicate. Include many guides for more difficulty.

26   Group Trust & Support

PROPS: 1 **TIME:** 5-10 **ALIAS:** Yurt Circle, CC-73
MOVE: 2 **SIZE:** 10-100 **ORIGIN:** Jim Schoel, Project Adv.

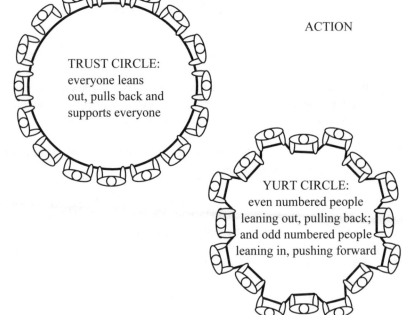

ACTION

TRUST CIRCLE:
everyone leans
out, pulls back and
supports everyone

YURT CIRCLE:
even numbered people
leaning out, pulling back;
and odd numbered people
leaning in, pushing forward

The position you are in (trust circle) represents group trust and support. Before you attempt a similar new structure (Yurt circle), let's first talk a little about trust and support.... Now that you have some of the basic concepts of trust and support, let's try a little risk taking. Stand up straight, relax the tension in the rope and in your mind imagine whether, in the next structure, you will be a risk taker (will lean forwards) or a supporter (will lean backwards). Realize that if everyone takes a risk (leans forward), you won't have enough support (leaning back) to keep the circular structure intact. Therefore, you will have to trust that enough people will choose to support rather than risk. In your mind, which are you: a risk taker or a supporter? If you are ready, let's slowly move toward your choice now!... Okay, I noticed several people changed their minds in mid-move and we need to validate that reversal of choice to risk is good, especially when support isn't present. Now, find a new optimal arrangement of supporters and risk takers. Any questions? Give everyone an opportunity to try both roles.

Action: People holding a rope circle take turns leaning in and out of the circle, testing their trust and support.

Intent: Trust, support, risk taking, coordination, and cooperation.

Note: This is a good activity to do early in a trust sequence. It can be done holding hands, but requires an even number of people this way. The use of a rope means it works with odd numbers of people: two can lean as one.

Equipment: A length of strong rope (at least 3' long for each person present), tied in a circle with a secure knot.

Setup: Ask everyone to place two hands on the rope and draw it back into a perfect circle. Once the shape has been formed, ask everyone to slowly lean back and put weight on the rope, or sit down and stand up if they can.

Task: To form a Yurt circle, where even numbered people pull back, and odd numbered people push forward.

Constraints: You must lean slowly and with control so that you can reverse your decision if necessary.

Safety: Use a wide open area, with soft ground, away from dangerous obstacles. Use a strong rope and knot.

Facilitation: The ideal arrangement is an equal number of people leaning both ways, alternating their directions. However, the group will find an arrangement that is best for them (maybe more than half leaning in, perhaps less) and whatever works is a good solution. Debrief for risk taking, trust and support. What does the rope represent?

Variations: Challenge the group to experiment with amounts and combinations. What is the minimum number of supporters needed so everyone else can take a risk? What is the maximum number of supporters that will prevent anyone from being able to take a risk? Put people inside the circle and try a sit down and stand up wave.

27   **Mutual Trust & Support**

PROPS: 0   **TIME:** 10-30   **ALIAS:** Wind in Willows, CC-52
MOVE: 3   **SIZE:** 6-12   **ORIGIN:** Classic

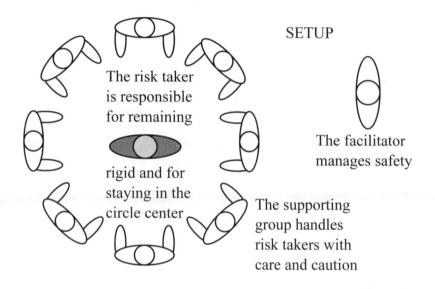

SETUP

The risk taker
is responsible
for remaining
rigid and for
staying in the
circle center

The facilitator
manages safety

The supporting
group handles
risk takers with
care and caution

This activity has two stances and four signals. The first stance is for the risk taker (RT); watch me demonstrate first. Stand straight and tall with your feet together and body rigid. Next, reverse clasp your hands together and invert them up beneath your chin. This is the ready-to-risk position for the RT. Try that without actually leaning.... The second stance is for the supporting group (SG); watch me demonstrate first. Stand with one foot ahead and to the side of the other, with feet about shoulder width apart, and knees slightly bent to protect your lower back. Hold your hands up and forward ready to support the head and shoulders of the RT. Try that without actually supporting.... Now we need to learn the safety signals for both roles. They go like this: RT = "Am I safe?" SG (together) = "YES, you're safe!" RT = "I'm ready to take a risk!" SG (together) = "We're here to support you!" Okay let's practice these.... Once both stances have been adopted and all signals have been spoken, then we can begin each round of this activity. Any questions?... Okay, let's have our first volunteer!

Action: People pass around and care for the safety of a rigid person leaning over in the center of a tight circle.

Intent: Trust, support, risk taking, coordination, communication, and cooperation.

Note: Do NOT conduct this activity, unless properly trained in its operation. Prior participation is NOT adequate training! If not qualified to lead this activity, obtain the expertise of someone who is well qualified. The brief description that follows is no substitute for a lack of training or experience with trust activities.

Equipment: None. However, a bag is useful to collect people's jewelry and sharp pocket contents for safety.

Setup: Gather everyone in to a tight circle standing shoulder to shoulder. Stand in the middle of the circle (only to demonstrate, do NOT participate in this activity). Explain that everyone will all have the choice to stand in the center of the group, to lean forwards into the arms of the group, and to be passed carefully around the circle.

Task: Take turns leaning in the center of the circle and being passed around the circle with care and caution.

Constraints: No one risks before signals are completed, and signals don't begin until both stances are adopted.

Safety: Allow people to pass their turn if they prefer and permit them to be challenged by their choice. As the facilitator, be vigilant about the accuracy of the stances and signals: stop and repeat instructions if necessary. As the SG get used to their roles, they tend to get rougher and escalate the RT's risk. Demand that they act gently.

Facilitation: Debrief for risk taking, fears, trust, and support issues. Discuss other related topics that arise.

Variations: Activity #28 is a more intense version, requiring extreme care by facilitators.

28   Coworker Trust & Support

PROPS: 4   **TIME:**   30-60   **ALIAS:**   Trust Fall, CC-53
MOVE: 4   **SIZE:**   8-12   **ORIGIN:** Classic

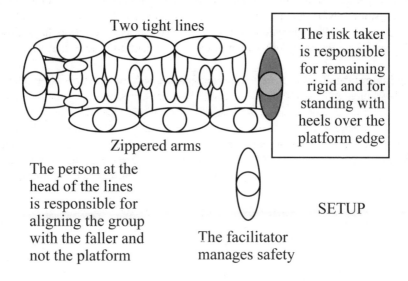

Two tight lines

The risk taker is responsible for remaining rigid and for standing with heels over the platform edge

Zippered arms

The person at the head of the lines is responsible for aligning the group with the faller and not the platform

The facilitator manages safety

SETUP

This activity has two stances and four signals. The first stance is for the risk taker (RT); watch me demonstrate first. Stand straight and tall with your feet together, ankles over the platform edge and body arched well back. Next, reverse clasp your hands together and invert them up beneath your chin. This is the ready-to-risk position for the RT. Try that without falling.... The second stance is for the supporting group (SG); watch me demonstrate first. Stand with one foot ahead and to the side of the other, with feet about shoulder width apart, and knees slightly bent to protect the lower back. Hold your forearms level with the ground, fingers together and palms up, ready to catch the RT's body. Try that without catching.... Now lets make tighten up the two lines facing one another, with your level arms interlocked like teeth on a zipper. Stand shoulder to shoulder, with two hands in the belly of the person across from you. Good. Lastly, we need to learn the safety signals for both roles. They go like this: RT = "Am I safe?" SG (together) = "YES, you're safe!" RT = "I'm ready to take a risk!" SG (together) = "We're here to support you!" Okay let's practice these.... Once both stances have been adopted and all signals have been spoken correctly, we can begin each individual fall sequence. Any questions?... Okay, let's have our first volunteer!

Action: In two parallel lines, people catch and care for the safety of a person falling backwards off a platform.

Intent: Trust, support, risk taking, coordination, communication, and cooperation.

Note: Do NOT conduct this activity, unless properly trained in its operation. Prior participation is NOT adequate training! If not qualified to lead this activity, obtain the expertise of someone who is well qualified. The brief description that follows is no substitute for a lack of training or experience with trust activities.

Equipment: This activity requires a specially constructed platform (or suitable substitute no more than 4' off the ground). The platform surface should be located at the average elbow height of the group performing the activity.

Setup: Collect people's jewelry and sharp objects. Form two lines of people facing one another with the lines perpendicular to the platform. Stand at the head of the two lines farthest from the platform (but definitely do NOT participate in this activity). Explain that everyone will all have the chance and the choice to stand on the platform and fall backwards into the specially arranged arms of the group. Their arms will be arranged like a zipper.

Task: Take turns falling from the platform in the prescribed fashion and into the zippered arms of the group.

Constraints: No one risks before signals are completed, and signals don't begin until both stances are adopted.

Safety: Allow people to pass if they prefer, highlighting challenge by choice. Be vigilant about the accuracy of the stances and signals: stop and repeat instructions whenever they miss a step in the sequence and then start over. After the SG have caught a RT, they tend to relax and may drop RT after catching. Remind them to pay attention.

Facilitation: Debrief for risk taking, fears, trust, and support issues. Discuss other related topics that arise.

Variations: Activity #27 is a less intense version, but still requires care from facilitators.

29   Completing Projects

PROPS: 1 **TIME:** 10-30 **ALIAS:** Tangrams, SB-129
MOVE: 0 **SIZE:** 7-21 **ORIGIN:** Classic

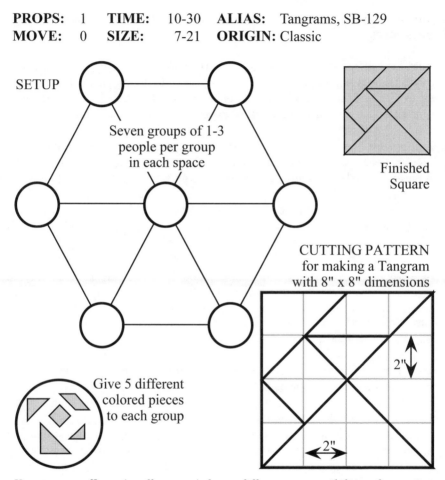

SETUP

Seven groups of 1-3
people per group
in each space

Finished
Square

CUTTING PATTERN
for making a Tangram
with 8" x 8" dimensions

Give 5 different
colored pieces
to each group

Your seven offices (small groups) have different responsibilities for various information in our company-wide project (5 pieces of a puzzle). You can see the way in which information flows among our company offices (7 space hexagonal area). The information you have combines to form identical finished projects (make several of the same large squares). When your office is finished with information, you may pass it to the next office in the chain (only along connecting lines), but you may not request information from another office (they will send it if and when they are ready). Unfortunately, no one in any offices speak the same languages (so this will all be done non-verbally). In your office, finish as many projects as you can before the 20 minute deadline. Any questions?

Action: 7 small groups of people trade pieces of a puzzle until 5 squares are completed (2 groups go without).

Intent: Sharing and sacrifice, communication, and competition versus cooperation.

Note: Any five puzzles will do, however, the Tangram designs are versatile and can be used in other activities.

Equipment: 5 different colored sets of Tangrams (cut up 8"x8" paper or cardboard). Tape for marking areas.

Setup: Mark out a hexagonal area with tape (as shown in the diagram). Split the big group into 7 small groups (of 1-3 people) put in each of 7 spaces. Shuffle all 35 Tangram pieces and divide these equally among 7 groups.

Task: For all 7 groups to make 5 squares (8"x8") out of puzzle pieces, without overlapping, folding or tearing.

Constraints: Must be conducted nonverbally. You may give away any puzzle piece to the nearest group (along the lines shown), but you may not take pieces from others nor indicate a desire to be given pieces by others.

Safety: Watch out: since the role of color is deliberately omitted, some people may argue over specific colors.

Facilitation: If the whole company is to succeed, at least two groups have to give up all their pieces and fail to finish their own projects. One solution involves the centrally located group receiving all 35 pieces, making 5 squares, and sending these back to the other groups. Debrief for sharing, sacrifice, collaboration, and teamwork.

Variations: Instead of making squares, ask each group to build a different silhouette like the cat, horse, bird, rider or runner diagrammed in activity #30 or create another design using the same colored pieces.

30 Replicating from Blueprints

PROPS: 2   **TIME:** 20-30   **ALIAS:** Le Cav (the cave), FSII-16
MOVE: 1   **SIZE:** 5-15   **ORIGIN:** Pat Rastall

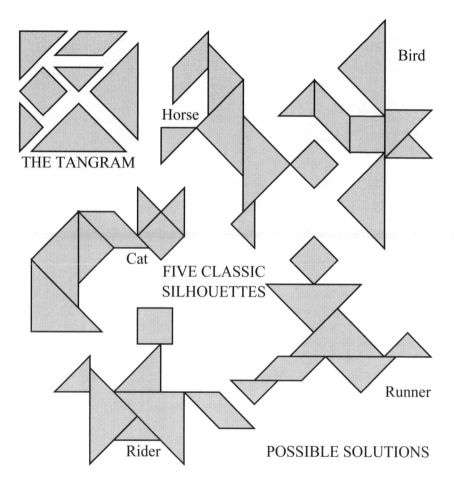

As your customer, I would like you to replicate a version of our latest product according to the blueprint (classic silhouette drawing) that you have 5 minutes to examine.... Now that you have detailed knowledge about the finished version, here are the replication materials (hand them the Tangram pieces). Unfortunately, the actual replication process has to be conducted in a darkroom in order to prevent damage to the product (so put on these blindfolds now). I need to have the final product replicated within the next 15 minutes. Any questions?

Action: Group studies a model (or photo of one) and then must replicate it from memory while blindfolded.

Intent: Communication, cooperation, and dealing with different perspectives of the same interpreted vision.

Note: If a square Tangram was used in activity #29, it will not be worth using again, choose a silhouette instead.

Equipment: One set of a 7 piece Tangram (or suitable other puzzle) and one blueprint like drawing of a classic silhouette (five choices are shown below or create a unique one) for each group. Blindfolds for everyone.

Setup: Explain to the group that this activity involves blindfolds (or a totally dark room) and let individuals choose in advance whether to participate. Provide a drawing of the classic silhouette and allow the group to study and discuss it for five minutes. If they are given an actual puzzle, allow them to handle it and learn the solution.

Task: While blindfolded, replicate a model that has been committed to common memory before time runs out.

Constraints: You must remain blindfolded for the duration of the replication process. Adhere to all time limits.

Safety: If people are uncomfortable wearing blindfolds, consider placing the group into a totally dark room. Always permit people to observe instead.

Facilitation: Feel free to demand ongoing updates from the group and negotiate with them if they need extra time (have them add value in some manner for each extra minute received). The interesting aspect of this activity is how people will see different content in the same drawing. Discuss these different perspectives and visions. Debrief how people dealt with these differences and whether they were willing to compromise in some small way

Variations: Substitute building blocks or construction toys for the Tangram. Instead of a drawing, share an actual blueprint or photograph of the model that details the construction. Prepare these in advance of the activity. For an easier activity, use the square Tangram (if not already used once) instead of the classic silhouettes above.

31   Disassembly & Reassembly

PROPS: 2   **TIME:** 30-60   **ALIAS:** The Window, NEW
MOVE: 1   **SIZE:** 10-20   **ORIGIN:** Australian Facilitators, S.P.

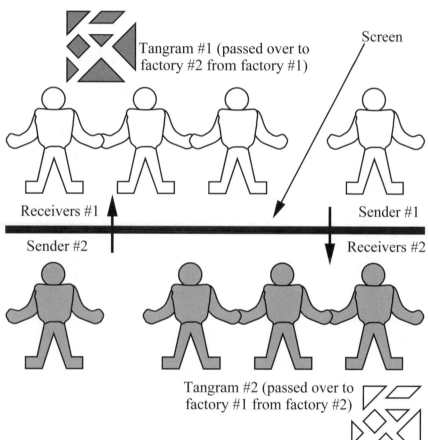

Tangram #1 (passed over to factory #2 from factory #1)

Screen

Receivers #1

Sender #1

Sender #2

Receivers #2

Tangram #2 (passed over to factory #1 from factory #2)

ACTION: After the exchange

Your two factories (half groups) are separated by a great distance (this screen). This prevents you from seeing what is happening at the other factory (don't peek), but you can communicate by phone (talk through the screen). You have 10 minutes to study and disassemble your prototype (Tangram). Then its components must be shipped to the other factory (exchanged under the screen) and both factories will have a further 20 minutes to reassemble the two prototypes, using information given by the other factory over the phone (through the screen). Any questions?

Action: Two groups attempt to disassemble and reassemble exchanged puzzles while talking through a screen.

Intent: Communication, cooperation, trust, problem solving, and group roles.

Note: This activity uses the silhouettes diagrammed in activity #30, or substitute any types of puzzles.

Equipment: Two sets of Tangrams (or puzzles) and a large tarp (with string or poles to help suspend it).

Setup: Hang the tarp vertically so that its bottom edge rests on the floor. Put preassembled Tangrams or puzzles on either side of the tarp and on the ground. Split the group in half and situate each half on either side of the tarp.

Task: To study, disassemble, and pass a puzzle beneath the tarp, and then tell the others how to reassemble it.

Constraints: You may not peek around the tarp, but you can talk through it. Only one exchange (passing pieces underneath the tarp) is permitted after your study period. Total time limit is 30 minutes (10 for disassembly and 20 for reassembly). Decide if groups will be able to use resources like pen or pencil and paper to assist them.

Safety: Be certain the tarp is well supported and that the support structure is well secured.

Facilitation: Once time has expired, lift the tarp and allow each group to see what the others have assembled. If the groups plan together for the first ten minutes and divide roles into disassemblers/senders of information and reassemblers/receivers, then communication will flow well. Watch for interference of information flow by one or the other. Debrief for miscommunications and accuracy of information. Discuss other teamwork lessons learned.

Variations: Have the groups disassemble and reassemble some unknown object that has something to do with their business (like actual car engines, computer components, and office buildings or products made from toy blocks). Eliminate the screen, separate the groups, and permit them to communicate by radios, phones or walkie-talkies.

32   Building a New Structure

PROPS: 2   **TIME:** 30-60   **ALIAS:** Blindfolded Tent, IG-37
MOVE: 2   **SIZE:** 5-10   **ORIGIN:** Outward Bound

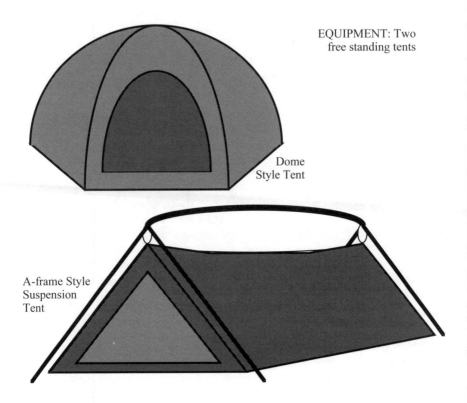

EQUIPMENT: Two
free standing tents

Dome
Style Tent

A-frame Style
Suspension
Tent

*Your group is attempting to restructure itself without the aid of a facilitator
and this lack of assistance stops you from seeing the bigger picture (so you are
blindfolded). The task is to build a new structure for your group (set up a tent)
using the resources available to you (bag at your feet) and without any help from a
facilitator. Once your new structure is complete, your group should see how well
it fits (get inside the tent). Any questions?*

Action: While wearing blindfolds, the entire group sets up a tent and then gathers inside it.

Intent: Communication, cooperation, trust, leadership, problem solving, and independence from a facilitator.

Note: This is an old activity meant to mimic putting up a tent in the dark without flashlights.

Equipment: One blindfold for each person and a free standing tent (large enough to get the whole group inside). Free standing tents (like domes or A-frame suspensions) that do not require any stakes to be driven into the ground.

Setup: Ask people to put on their blindfolds and, once they cannot see, bring out the tent and place it at their feet.

Task: To set up the tent and get the entire group inside the tent while fully blindfolded.

Constraints: Although participants are blindfolded, they may speak with one another.

Safety: Teach people the bumpers up position (hands up and held forward of their shoulders). Watch out for people walking blind (clear obstacles from their way) and carrying long tent poles (that might spear or poke others).

Facilitation: Discuss arising issues and how the change comes from the group's effort not the facilitator's.

Variations: For greater difficulty, ask for nonverbal communication. For greater ease, allow one person to be sighted and to give directions based on reading the instructions that came with the tent (assuming these exist).

33   Shaping the Organization

PROPS: 2   **TIME:** 10-30   **ALIAS:** Blind Polygon, CC-81
MOVE: 1   **SIZE:** 4-40   **ORIGIN:** Outward Bound

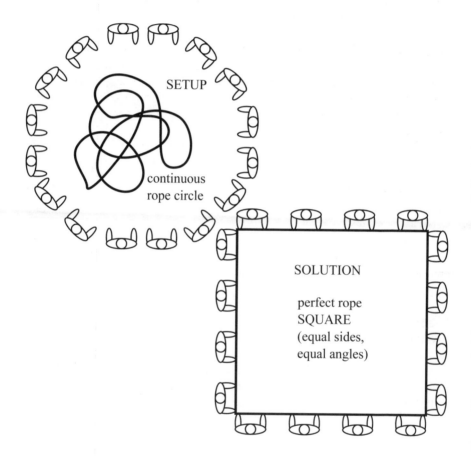

SETUP

continuous
rope circle

SOLUTION

perfect rope
SQUARE
(equal sides,
equal angles)

*In this activity, we will be shaping the organization (indicate the pile of rope).
Each of us knows in our own minds what we think the organization should look
like, but we are frequently blind to one another's visions when starting out (please
put your blindfolds on now). It takes everyone to share their vision openly and to
the shape this new organization into a square (with precisely equal length of sides
and 90 degree angles at the four corners). Any questions?*

Action: Blindfolded group attempts to create complex and precise shapes with the circle of rope they are holding.

Intent: Quality, accuracy, communication, cooperation, trust, problem solving, and leadership.

Note: The next activity (#34) is very similar to this, but uses more complex shapes, without wearing blindfolds.

Equipment: One blindfold for each participant and one very long rope (at least 3' of length for each participant).

Setup: Tie a knot to join the ends of the rope into a continuous circle. Place the rope in a pile on the ground.

Task: To make a square (equal length sides and right angled corners) from the rope circle while blindfolded.

Constraints: Angles of corners and lengths of sides for the square (or other shape chosen) must be precise.

Safety: Ask everyone to adopt the bumpers up position while holding the rope in front of them. If people are uncomfortable wearing blindfolds, ask them to remove their blindfold, and quietly step out to observe the activity. Remove any dangerous obstacles in advance and/or spot people who might be moving toward any such dangers.

Facilitation: Most groups simply make a four sided object that is a far cry from square. If this should happen, have them take a quick peek at the result and ask: "Is this a square?" If the quality is not up to their standards, allow them to continue until they are satisfied with the final version. One solution is to fold the rope into four parallel lengths (in order to get equal lengths) and then to pull those out from the bends to get the right angled corners. In some cases, a diamond (uneven angles) may be the closest they will get to a square. Discuss quality, accuracy satisfaction, and whether they double checked their square. Debrief for communication, cooperation, and leadership.

Variations: Any number of other shapes (triangle, hexagon, pentagon, etc.) are more difficult than a square and more appropriate for larger groups. With smaller groups, provide noodles and ask them to make 3D shapes like a cube or pyramid (UYN-116). The easiest version permits one person to see and direct the blindfolded others.

34   **Product Logo Duplication**

PROPS: 1   **TIME:** 10-20   **ALIAS:** Sighted Star/House, ZG-78
MOVE: 1   **SIZE:**   5-10   **ORIGIN:** Sam Sikes, Simon Priest

EQUIPMENT:
Two shapes to
use (draw these
without giving
easy answers)

You have two new logos for products you are soon to be rolling out. In this experience, you will need to duplicate each logo using <u>all</u> of the available resources (indicate the rope). Once you have come in contact with the resources (rope), you will need to maintain contact until the logo is completed. Any questions? The first logo looks like this (draw the star as diagrammed).... Once the star has been created, draw the house as diagrammed, and draw it in such a way that you do not try to keep continuous contact with the drawing utensil, since this gives away the answer. Also, if the house is created with the rope doubled back in any place, emphasize the error by drawing the shape the group has created, but do not emphasize a lack of continuity as this leads to the solution. If observers want to show they have figured it out, ask everyone if they would like to switch to 5 new participants.

Action: Using a long loop of rope to create two shapes (the star is possible and the house is not possible).

Intent: Making assumptions (the knot must be untied to make the house) and stepping away from problems.

Note: This is ideal for 5 people. Ask the rest of the group to observe or to substitute in during the activity.

Equipment: One long continuous rope (with sufficient obstacle free space to move around and arrange shapes).

Setup: In front of the group, tie the rope into a loop by knotting the ends together, and then toss it on the ground.

Task: The house can only be created if the rope is untied. Prior success (with not needing to untie the rope for the star) tends to discourage people from thinking outside the box and untying the rope for their second shape.

Constraints: Don't mention the knot can be untied unless someone asks directly. If asked indirectly, simply repeat the rules: "You cannot let go of the rope and you must use all the rope to make the shape!"

Safety: Provide sufficient space for stretching out and folding back the rope loops. Move dangerous obstacles.

Facilitation: Discuss what happens when one makes assumptions (ASS U ME). If observers identify the crux assumption much earlier than participants, discuss how separation from a problem aids in its ultimate solution. Other topics for the debrief include problem solving, communication, cooperation, leadership, and teamwork.

Variations: To make the task more difficult, constrain people from switching positions or have them do the task nonverbally. The shapes are extremely difficult, if done blindfolded (see activity #33). People often need visual feedback to succeed. Other shapes that can be used include polygons, letters of the alphabet, and short words.

35   **Producing a Prototype**

PROPS: 2   **TIME:**   30-60   **ALIAS:**   Team Triangle, BM-148
MOVE: 1   **SIZE:**   10-20   **ORIGIN:** Simon Priest

EQUIPMENT:
Sample blueprint

Using
ALL THE ROPE
provided, form a perfect
equilateral triangle with all
three angles of 60 degrees and
all three sides equal in length to a 2"
tolerance error. You may untangle the
rope, but you may NOT untie any knots that
make the rope a continuous loop. Any questions?

You are salespeople and may speak freely with one another or ask questions of me as your customer. Here are my blueprints for a prototype that I would like your company to produce in the next 20 minutes. Since you speak different languages, you cannot talk directly to any other employees. However, you can nonverbally communicate with the managers and they will pass messages between you and the workers. Any questions?

Action: Blind group forms a triangle with information communicated by nonverbal group through translators.

Intent: Communication (within and among groups), power and empowerment in the problem solving process.

Note: Forming a triangle can be replaced by any complex puzzle such as Tangrams from activities #29 and #30.

Equipment: One long (10'-30') piece of rope, 3 blindfolds, and 3 separated areas (two rooms and a hallway).

Setup: Break the group up into 3 subgroups: blind workers, mute salespeople, and full faculty managers (let people pick a role). Place the blind workers in one room. Have them wear their blindfolds, remain in this room and await further instructions from management. Knot the rope ends together and leave the formed loop with them. Place the full faculty managers in the hallway between the two rooms. Explain they will act as subgroup intermediaries. Tell them not to leave the hallway and to wait for additional directions from sales. Place the mute salespeople in the other room. Indicate that they are to stay in the room and then present the activity frame or introduction opposite.

Task: Via the intermediaries, the mute group have to get the blind group to accurately create a triangle from rope.

Constraints: No one may leave their areas (rooms or hallway). Mute sales may not speak to other subgroups. Other subgroups may speak to anyone. Facilitator (customer) decides whether tolerances have been met or surpassed.

Safety: Protect blindfolded people by removing obstacles from their room. Close the door to the other room if any conversations within the mute subgroup can be overheard by others. Remind people to stay in their areas.

Facilitation: Debrief for some of the more common miscommunications in this experience: statement inaccuracy and details; not sharing the bigger picture; and not allowing workers to be part of the problem solving process.

Variations: This is a great activity for video conferencing: disable audio-in or audio-out for managers and video-in or video-out for workers. As a customer feel free to negotiate with the sales team, request regular updates on progress, and if needs change, by all means modify the order in mid-production by adding new requirements or adjusting the existing tolerances.

36   **Factory Pilot Testing**

PROPS: 3   **TIME:** 60-120   **ALIAS:** Identical Objects, NEW
MOVE: 2   **SIZE:** 10-50   **ORIGIN:** Australian Facilitators, S.P.

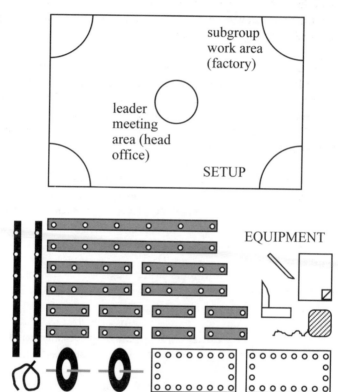

You are factory leaders and you can call a leadership meeting at the head office (center of field or gym) at any time. Your task is to have your 4 factories (corners) each create an exact copy of a transportation vehicle using the raw materials you have in stock. This vehicle will safely carry a cargo through a test track with two drivers (pushers). Unfortunately, the factories are located in different corners of the world and so cannot communicate verbally with one another due to cultural differences. However, you may confer with one another as often as you like, by simply walking over here and waiting for the others to attend the meeting (you may not yell out to them). Once you have finished four vehicles within the next 60 minutes, we will all gather here at the head office for a quality comparison, then we will pilot test the vehicles using the factory leaders (you) as cargo! Any questions?

Action: Four subgroups create four copies of the same transport device to carry their leaders.

Intent: Quality control, communication, leadership, collaboration, and planning.

Note: Final products are usually wheelchairs, wheelbarrows or wheeled stretchers. However, the final product can be almost anything. For example, the materials below can also be used to build a catapult (activity #93).

Equipment: Four materials sets each composed of: 2 wheels with axles; two 6' long 2"x2" boards (with 0.25" holes drilled at various places along their lengths); 2"x4" boards (two 8', four 4', and eight 2' long; also with 0.25" holes); two 2'x4' pieces of 0.5" thick plywood (with 0.25" holes drilled around its edges); a ball of twine; a knife; 3' of bungee cord; paper and pen (optional); and a large space like a playing field or gymnasium.

Setup: Put one materials set in each corner of the field (gym). Divide the larger group into 4 smaller subgroups and ask each group to elect a leader. Send the groups to their respective corners and gather 4 leaders at the center.

Task: To build four exact copies of a transportation vehicle that will allow two pushers to carry one person.

Constraints: Subgroups may not speak to one another; only leaders may do this and only at the head office in the center of the area.

Safety: Obviously check the finished products for similarity, stability (shake them roughly), strength (test with the weight of a facilitator), and steerability (turns on a dime) before allowing subgroups to go to the test track. Substitute nuts, bolts and washers to fit drilled holes, if concerned about using knives, string or bungee cords.

Facilitation: Subgroups can see and overhear what some of the other subgroups are doing and this can present interesting rumors that may hamper the overall effort. Discuss leadership and issues related to quality control.

Variations: Distribute materials unevenly to see if sharing or equalizing of resources occurs among subgroups. Give radios or phones to the leaders and prevent them from returning to the center to meet. Substitute other team projects for the transportation vehicle (#91-#97). Most activities can utilize this concept of teams working in parallel as a way to reduce one large group into several smaller manageable subgroups (with at least one facilitator for each subgroup).

37   **Project Setbacks**

PROPS: 2   **TIME:** 20-40   **ALIAS:** Minefield, BBA-52
MOVE: 1   **SIZE:** 2-20   **ORIGIN:** Unknown

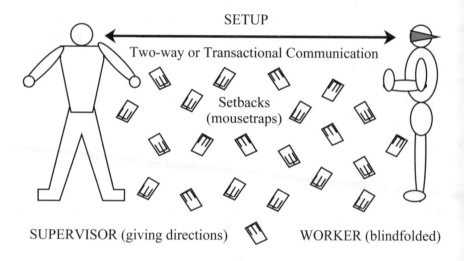

SETUP

Two-way or Transactional Communication

Setbacks
(mousetraps)

SUPERVISOR (giving directions)   WORKER (blindfolded)

In front of you is a project area fraught with setbacks (mousetraps). This is your first time doing this work, so you are blind to many of these setbacks (so please put on your blindfolds now). With the help of a partner who has done this work before (who can see), you will be expected to get through the project as quickly as possible without setback (get to the other side without stepping on a mousetrap). If you have a setback (step on a trap), then you may continue, but after recovering (stand still for one minute). However, if you can pick up a phone or keyboard, you can contact your supervisor or check your database for valuable information (remove your blindfold and discuss strategy with your partner for one minute, without moving during this time). If you lose track of the project (step across a boundary and leave the area) you will need to start again. Any questions?

Action: Blindfolded people navigate their way through obstacles (mousetraps) with directions from partners.

Intent: Two-way or transactional communication, trust, support, and cooperation versus competition.

Note: Mousetraps are used in this activity for surprising effect. As long as closed-toe footwear is worn, injury potential is minimal.

Equipment: Blindfolds for half the group, a rope or tape (for marking boundaries), about 100 mousetraps (or other objects such as bean bags or paper sheets), and a few extra things like cell phones or computer keyboards.

Setup: Use rope or tape to mark out an area. Arm mousetraps and distribute them (or other objects) evenly and randomly around this area. Put cell phones or keyboards somewhere in the middle. Ask the group to pick partners and for one partner to be blindfolded. Send non-blindfolded partners to the opposite side of the area.

Task: To get through the obstacles by using a partner's advice, avoiding penalties and seeking rewards.

Constraints: If you set off a mousetrap (or step on an object), you must stand still for one minute. If you touch the phone or keyboard, you get 60 seconds to look around without your blindfold on. You may talk strategy, but not advance.

Safety: If anyone is uncomfortable wearing a blindfold, ask them to remove it and be an observer for rest of the activity. No bare feet or open-toed footwear permitted. In addition to the obvious obstacles, blindfolded people can run into one another, so encourage bumpers up. Watch out for the occasional excited person who may rush.

Facilitation: A big concern is the noise caused by other's communications. Discuss how people focused in on their partner's voice. Debrief for competition versus cooperation and for miscommunications leading to setbacks.

Variations: Form three person groups: a worker, a supervisor, and a manager. The supervisor looks away from the area toward the manager. The manager observes the walker and hand signals the supervisor, who tells the worker which way to go. Make the minefield area 3D by adding horizontal wires and hanging obstacles.

38   Getting There on Time

PROPS: 1   **TIME:** 10-20   **ALIAS:** Photo Finish, ZG-114
MOVE: 2   **SIZE:** 10-30   **ORIGIN:** Sam Sikes, Rudy Pucel

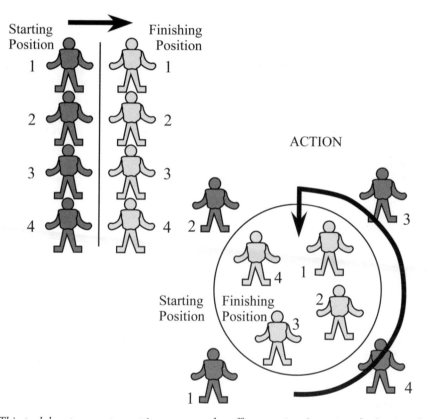

This task has two parts: getting to a nearby office meeting (crossing the line) and getting to a distant team-building retreat (entering a circle). The two criteria for success in this task are just-in-time simultaneous arrivals (all cross the rope at the exact same instant) and no bumping or inconveniencing others as you arrive (don't touch one another). Any questions?... Okay, let's get over to that office meeting (cross to the other side by standing as close as you like to the rope).... Now that we've decided our limits for arriving at the meeting have been reached (circle the rope and tie its ends together), we can get over to that team building retreat that is all the way across town (walk half way around the circle, in the same direction, to the exact opposite side and then simultaneously cross over the rope into the circle).

Action: Group attempts to move as one simultaneously across a linear (and then a circular) boundary.

Intent: Coordination, frustration, blaming behavior, time-management, and cooperation.

Note: This also combines activities known collectively as Hut 2, 3, 4 (FSII-21) and Ameoba (FSIII-27).

Equipment: A 60' length of rope (or a natural linear feature). Optional video camera to give instant feedback.

Setup: Lay the rope out in a straight line and assemble the group on one side of the rope. Position the camera.

Task: Cross the rope at the exact same moment (over a line, then into a circle) and without touching one another.

Constraints: All cross at the same time and without physical contact. If either are not achieved, try once again.

Safety: Spot people who get bumped off balance. If people disagree about their performance, consult the video record.

Facilitation: Let them take full responsibility for organizing how they will do this, especially calling signals and saying "GO!" Transition from the stationary line to the moving circle at the time when the group decides they have done their absolute best so far and are ready to progress. Debrief for frustration instead of performance. Rather than calling out all their errors, ask the group to establish their own quality control. This can provide remarkable insights into ethical choices and peer pressure associated with a very difficult task that initially seemed so simple.

Variations: Add an inner circle and after they enter from outside the outer circle, ask them to continue walking the path between both circles and then step out together after another half circuit. Change the shape from a circle to something with tighter corners like a square or triangle. Allow physical contact for easier simultaneous movement, or have them start a few feet away from the rope line or rope circle for greater difficulty of movement.

39   **Organization Orientation**

PROPS: 1   **TIME:** 20-40   **ALIAS:** Turnstiles, BBA-116
MOVE: 3   **SIZE:** 5-40   **ORIGIN:** Karl Rohnke

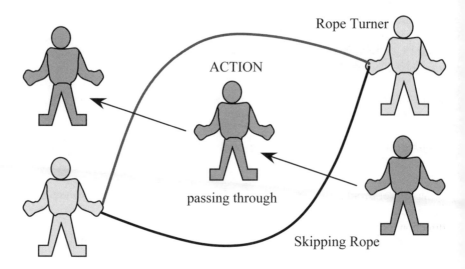

All employees have to go through your organizational orientation program at least once (everyone passes through the turning rope, but don't have to jump), graduating either on their own or with the aid of others in the group (more than one person can pass during each turn). The program organizers (rope turners) determine the pace of the program (speed and direction of turns) and also end up eventually participating in every program (rope turners must also pass through). Since your organization and this program are team-oriented, if a program fails to get full participation, or if one person doesn't graduate, then everyone will have to start over in the next program (if rope makes a full turn without someone passing through or if someone is caught by the rope during a passage, then everyone must start over). Programs run continuously (so the rope is always turning). Any questions?

Action: Group attempts to pass through a turning rope (together or one by one) without getting hit by the rope.

Intent: Coordination, frustration, blaming behavior, planning, cooperation, and ethics.

Note: This activity also incorporates variations from Hop Box (QS-167) and further builds on activity #38.

Equipment: A 30' length of (retired climbing) rope to be used as a skipping rope.

Setup: Ask 2 people to hold the rope ends, pull it out until it is straight, and begin turning it like a skipping rope.

Task: To get everyone through the turning rope at least once without missing a turn or getting caught by the rope.

Constraints: Jumps are optional. Pass through alone, with others, or all together, as long as everyone passes through the turning rope once (including the rope turners, who can switch roles as necessary). If the rope makes a turn without someone getting through, or catches someone trying to pass through, everyone must start over. Turners decide how fast or slow to turn the rope and in which direction it turns (toward or away from the group).

Safety: Do this on a soft surface with a firm footing (dry grass instead of loose gravel) in case people trip up and fall down. Stretch large muscle groups and practice jumping in advance of rushing in to skip.

Facilitation: Some groups may pass the majority through in one turn, but then have trouble including both rope turners. Often, trading positions with rope turners can lead to errors that have everyone starting over again. Have them manage their own quality control. Debrief for planning, frustration, blaming, and ethics.

Variations: Have more than one rope turning (like four in a square) and provide a choice of route for greater ease or mandate all passages for more difficulty. Time the event, ignore misses, and restart only captured people.

40   **Competing for Customers**

PROPS: 2   **TIME:** 20-30   **ALIAS:** Insanity, EM-94
MOVE: 3   **SIZE:** 10-40   **ORIGIN:** Sam Sikes

Central Hula
Hoop (filled
with all the   SETUP
objects
to start)

Hula Hoops
(30' apart)

COLLABORATIVE SOLUTION
(put all hoops together
around all the objects)

*You are four separate sales groups (hoops) who sell different services to the public
(center hoop). You are interested in maximizing your market share by selling
to as many customers (objects) as you can this quarter (next 2 minutes). You
must handle one customer at a time (carry one object only). You should proceed
with caution (shuffle, don't walk or run). Handle customers with great care (no
throwing or dropping objects) in order to ensure the most sales (get the maximum
objects inside your hoop). After all customers have been sold their first service
(center hoop is empty), you may begin engaging customers from other groups
and this may lead to second sales (you can take those objects back to your hoop).
Once you have made any sale, there is no need to defend customers or impede
other's success (do not block your hoop or harass others). Any questions? GO!*

Action: Groups compete to transfer objects to their hula hoops (instead of sharing objects by moving the hoops).

Intent: Competition versus cooperation, ethical behaviors, planning, frustration of futility, and communication.

Note: This is NOT an activity where people should be allowed to run (or even walk, which can lead to running).

Equipment: Five hula hoops and a wide variety of objects (balls, bean bags or paper scraps) about 3 per person.

Setup: Put one hula hoop in the middle and the other four in a square, each about 30' away. Fill the central hoop with all the objects. Teach everyone to shuffle (walk without feet breaking contact with the ground); this can prevent running. Divide everyone into four groups and send a group to each of the four remaining hula hoops.

Task: To get the maximum number of objects in your designated hula hoop before time runs out.

Constraints: Once all objects are gone from the center hoop, you may begin taking objects from other hoops. You may not defend your hoop or prevent objects being taken from it. You may only carry one object at a time and may not throw or drop objects. Do not harass others. Move only by shuffling: no running or fast walking.

Safety: To reduce collisions, demand shuffling (constant foot to ground contact): NO running or fast walking.

Facilitation: Start the activity immediately without time for the groups to plan. After 2 minutes, call STOP and announce the next round, but this time give 3 minutes to plan. At some point, someone may ask if the hula hoops can be moved. Simply repeat the rules and avoid telling them that moving hoops is a collaborative solution. Debrief for cooperation and ethics. What does all five hoops together around every object represent at work?

Variations: For more frantic action, permit throwing objects and carrying more than one object at a time. For a larger group, simply add several more hula hoops around the outside (about 1 hoop for every 10 extra people).

41   Caring for Customers

PROPS: 2   **TIME:**   5-10   **ALIAS:** Lowering the Bar, NEW
MOVE: 1   **SIZE:**   5-20   **ORIGIN:** Mike Gass

SETUP AND ACTION

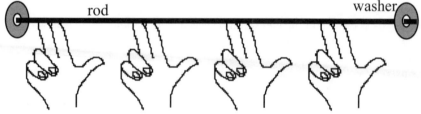

You are servicing your customers (indicate a rod) who have certain values (indicate the washers). While maintaining constant support of your customers (don't lose contact with the rod), move them in a very caring and responsible manner (keeping the rod level) toward meeting their needs (reaching the ground) without abandoning their values (dropping the washers). If you abandon the customers' values, then you will not be able to meet their needs and you will surely lose them and have to start over again with new ones. Any questions? Okay, GO!

Action: The group supports a horizontal rod and attempts to lower it to the ground, while keeping it level.

Intent: Addressing blaming behavior, conflict, cooperation, and coordination.

Note: In this activity, the rod tends to go up, despite one's best efforts to lower it: hence the blaming potential.

Equipment: One light 6' rod (like aluminum poles, fiberglass dowels or bamboo wands) and two large washers.

Setup: Put washers on the tip of each end of the rod and hold it horizontally at waist level. Ask people to take one hand, place two fingers together on their hand and keep the rod level by supporting it from underneath. Let go of the rod.

Task: Keep the rod level and lower it to the ground, despite an upward motion caused by supporting underneath.

Constraints: Only support from beneath with two fingers on one hand. Maintain contact with rod at all times. When you see a loss of contact, either remind them or ask them to begin again.

Safety: Watch out for any sharp ends. Encourage people to sit the rod in the crotch between their two fingers.

Facilitation: In dysfunctional groups, blaming is common and people can become very frustrated. Despite their best efforts to lower the rod, it continues to rise and they believe the group has a saboteur in its ranks. Debrief for blaming behavior and any other teamwork lessons that are evident. Watch out for serious conflict in the group.

Variations: Permit the use of both hands and more fingers. Provide tape for people who can't keep their two fingers together. Add blindfolds and nonverbal constraints (much harder). Try it without the washers (much easier).

42   **Warehouse Inventory**

PROPS: 1   **TIME:** 20-40   **ALIAS:** Key Punch, QS-169
MOVE: 3   **SIZE:** 10-30   **ORIGIN:** Australian Facilitators, S.P.

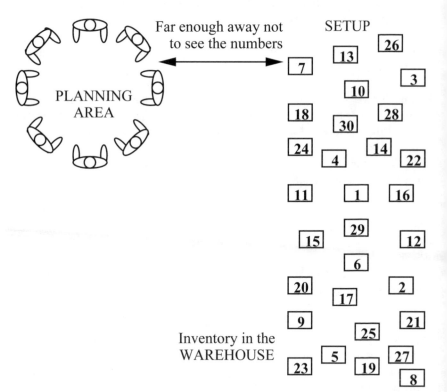

Over there, in your warehouse, you have thirty different products (spaces) comprising your inventory. These are consecutively numbered from 1 to 30, but will always be stored in random order. As a group, you have 30 minutes or 5 attempts to take stock of these products by covering each one in numerical order (actually put a foot or hand on the space to count it). Once started, an inventory must be completed in under 30 seconds. If you inventory a product out of sequence (touch a wrong number), then you lose one attempt, the inventory is rearranged (spaces shuffled) and you must start over. Plan again if you want to, but the clock continues to run. Since the warehouse is located by a noisy airport, you should do your planning and talking here, because you can't talk or hear one another over there (no talking once counting spaces). Any questions?... Time starts now!

Action: Group stepping on numbered squares in numerical sequence, without speaking and before time runs out.

Intent: Planning, timing, cooperation, communication, and problem solving.

Note: The classic version of this activity allows one person inside a marked area at a time; this version does not so as to avoid the relay running race approach.

Equipment: Thirty spaces (pages of paper) numbered 1-30. Two watches for timing might be helpful here.

Setup: Spread the numbered spaces randomly on the floor so that no space is more than 2' from the next one. Assemble the group in a distant location well away from specific spaces, but close enough to see the general area.

Task: To cover 30 randomly ordered spaces in sequence and under 30 seconds.

Constraints: Plan at a distant location with talking, but no talking near the thirty spaces. You are limited to 5 tries or 30 minutes (which ever expires first) and the clock is running during planning time. The error of touching a number out of order means starting over with a new arrangement of numbered spaces and the clock continues to run.

Safety: Ten people can cover thirty spaces with two feet and one hand each if the spaces are close enough to one another. Put the spaces closer together for smaller groups so no one has to stretch too far. If people are running back and forth between planning and inventory, offer to temporarily stop time so no one rushes and falls down while rushing across a long distance.

Facilitation: Some groups use almost all their time planning and then try 5 quick attempts in the last 5 minutes. Other groups will plan for a few minutes and then make an attempt in order to get valuable information to take back to another planning session. Discuss planning strategies and debrief for time management and cooperation.

Variations: For an interesting situation of coping with the unexpected, leave two numbers out (17 and 27) and double up on two numbers (26 and 29) instead. As long as there are still thirty numbers and still they range from 1 to 30, the facilitator can still state "the thirty numbers range from 1 to 30" without being dishonest or unethical. For an easier task, simply have people touching the 30 numbers in sequence, rather than having to cover them up. Use letters of the alphabet instead of numbers and have the group stamp out a keyword.

43   Smooth Shift Changes

PROPS: 1   **TIME:** 10-30   **ALIAS:** Don't Touch Me, QS-156
MOVE: 2   **SIZE:** 10-40   **ORIGIN:** American Facilitators, K.R.

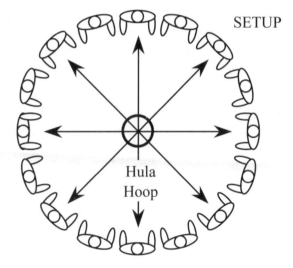

You are involved with a shift change at your manufacturing plant and are about to switch places with an assembly line buddy (identified partner). Only 30 seconds are available to change shifts (get to the other side) and during this time, each worker has to punch the time clock (step once in the central hula hoop) and hand off critical information to their buddy (perform a high-five move on the way past your partner). However, this must all be done without interfering with anyone else (no collisions with others, except the high-five contacts) and without any pauses (everyone must start moving together and keep moving: no stops once everyone has started moving). You have 5 practices to perform the shift change perfectly and 5 minutes to plan between practices. Any questions?

Action: Group must cross to the far side of a circle, by stepping in a hula hoop and without touching each other.

Intent: Coordination strategies, planning, continuous improvement, cooperation, communication, and trust.

Note: Do this activity in a wide open area with soft ground and without any dangerous obstacles.

Equipment: One hula hoop. Using a long piece of rope or masking tape (to mark the outer circle) is optional.

Setup: Place the hula hoop on the ground and gather the group around it in a large (arm lengths apart) circle. Ask each person to identify, make eye contact with, and point at a partner on the exact opposite side of the circle.

Task: To cross to the exact opposite side of the circle in 30 seconds, with one hoop step and a partner high-five.

Constraints: Once everyone starts to move together, no one must stop or touch anyone else on their way to the far side (excluding the high-fives). Contact or a stop means using one of your five attempts and planning again.

Safety: Expect more than one collision the first time the group tries to cross over and encourage bumpers up.

Facilitation: This is a deceptively difficult task for most groups. Either they bump into each other, or someone stops to avoid a collision, and everyone starts over with the loss of one try. Discuss the seemingly easy tasks at work and the role of practicing to continuously improve. Debrief for coordination, communication, and planning.

Variations: Staying with a continuous improvement theme, challenge the effective groups to get their time under 15 seconds. Skipping the high-five, and/or allowing people to stop moving if they want, makes this task easier.

44   **What Do You Stand For?**

PROPS: 0   **TIME:**   5-30   **ALIAS:** Lineups, SB-163
MOVE: 1   **SIZE:**   5-100   **ORIGIN:** Karl Rohnke, Simon Priest

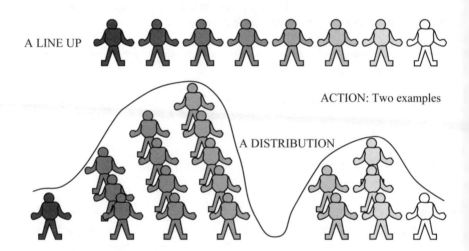

A LINE UP

ACTION: Two examples

A DISTRIBUTION

Without talking, I'd like you to line up according to how long you spend in the office each week.... Now that you appear to have finished shifting places, tell me about your workloads or free time.... Now I'd like you to distribute yourselves between always and never, on the basis of how often you are seen as a team player.

Action: Nonverbally, groups get in lines according to degrees of frequency, agreement, opinion or value.

Intent: Communication and generating discussion about uncomfortable topics.

Note: The difference between line ups and distributions: the former are straight lines (everyone must stand beside one another) and the latter can be bell curves (several people may occupy the same spot and some spaces may be left open). For this activity, begin with line ups according to time employed by the company or distance driven to work (or something equally benign). Once, they are comfortable with the process, have them do a distribution on more controversial topics like opinions about the corporate mission statement, agreement with company policies, importance of integrity, frequency of illnesses or absences, value given to paperwork procedures, or how personal energy levels are at that moment. Plan these topics well in advance.

Equipment: None (don't worry about the absence of a line to stand on, since the group will create one).

Setup: Assemble the group and ask them to line up or create a distribution on the basis of the above questions.

Task: To get in a lineup/distribution from lowest to highest, from shortest to longest, from closest to farthest, from least to most, from true to false, from never to always, from agree to disagree, or from important to unimportant.

Constraints: Do this nonverbally. If people want to reposition someone, encourage them to do so respectfully.

Safety: Consider emotional safety by offering the opportunity for people to say "I pass" on any question asked.

Facilitation: Line ups will often involve communication through a symbolic language (such as a number of fingers representing years employed or miles driven), but different languages will occasionally be spoken without realizing it (years or months, miles or minutes, and tens or units?). Discuss miscommunications. Distributions will have less symbolic communication (perhaps none at all), but provide permission for people to speak about their stances and positions.

Variations: For fun, try nonverbal shoe sizes (comparing feet), ages (people of the same age may not account for birth dates), salaries, heights, number of siblings, or ID numbers (the last four are worth doing blindfolded).

45   Project Management

PROPS: 4   **TIME:** 10-30   **ALIAS:** TP Shuffle, CC-112
MOVE: 2   **SIZE:** 6-12   **ORIGIN:** Karl Rohnke

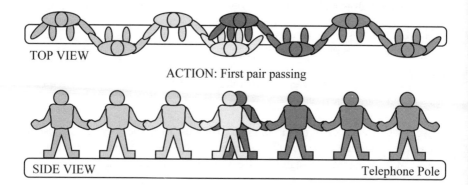

Your two departments (half groups) are managing the same project (log), but are working in two very different ways. One department is forward processing from beginning to end and the other is reverse processing from end to beginning as a double check. Inevitably, you will get in each other's way. When that happens, you will need to work together (to pass one another) without losing control over the project (stepping or slipping off). If anyone loses control, both departments will need to start over (begin again from this position). Any questions?

Action: Two half groups attempt to pass one another atop a horizontal log without slipping or stepping off.

Intent: Trust, support, cooperation, communication, asking for and offering help, and problem solving.

Note: The TP in TP Shuffle stands for Telephone Pole, which is normally laying on the ground surrounded by soft wood chips.

Equipment: A horizontal log (like a telephone pole) or a suitable substitute, placed about 1' above ground.

Setup: Ask people to take turns standing on the log. As they stand up, ask each one to tell the group about a behavior that they personally stand for in the group or that the group can rely on them to do consistently. Once everyone is on the log, split the group in half and ask the half groups to move to opposite ends of the log.

Task: To change sides of the log by passing by all of the other half and without stepping or slipping off the log.

Constraints: If you step or slip off onto ground, everyone must return to their starting positions to begin again.

Safety: Remove dangerous obstacles. Spot people as they pass. Remove jewelry and sharp pocket objects.

Facilitation: People who try to pass one another without external support, usually slip off, causing everyone to start over. Once they realize that support from the others (holding hands or bracing arms) passing becomes much easier. The next barrier to overcome is offering or accepting assistance. Debrief for giving and receiving help. Discuss trust, support, and cooperation. Did people follow through on the behaviors they stood for at the start?

Variations: Precede the passing with a line up (activity #44) on the log, and then have them pass one another into a new line up while staying on the log. Do activity #7 or #8 while on the log. Add nonverbal constraints to make the task more difficult. Adjust the penalty to only the faller or all of the faller's half group must start over from the log end (this adjustment lends itself to competition between half groups).

46   World Journey

PROPS: 4   **TIME:** 20-40   **ALIAS:** Quadjam, BB-39
MOVE: 2   **SIZE:** 8-16   **ORIGIN:** Craig Dobkin

The
Quadjam
(log square)
SETUP

In this activity, each of you will be expected to take your turn (move one at a time) to journey around the world (travelling one circuit around the log square) to visit your company's four continental headquarters (past all four corners) with the support of your co-workers (you must pass everyone). If you get lost in your travels (step or slip off the log), then you will need to restart your journey from the nearest headquarters that you just left (start from the last corner passed, no others need repeat their circuits). Due to the obvious language barriers, there is no point in speaking English with anyone you might meet along the way (no talking). Any questions?

Action: Each person completes a journey on a square of horizontal logs, passing everyone without slipping off.

Intent: Trust, support, cooperation, communication, asking for and offering help, and problem solving.

Note: This activity is a nice alternative to activity #45, because it provides more individual challenge with group support.

Equipment: A Quadjam: a square of four short horizontal logs at ground level and surrounded by wood chips.

Setup: Ask people to take turns standing on the logs, while sharing a team behavior that they stand for or that the group can consistently expect of them. Ask them to distribute themselves evenly around the log square.

Task: For everyone to make a complete circuit, by passing everyone and without stepping or slipping off a log.

Constraints: If you step or slip off, only you must return to the last corner. Conduct this activity non-verbally.

Safety: Remove dangerous obstacles. Spot people as they pass. Remove jewelry and sharp pocket objects.

Facilitation: As in the previous activity (#45), external support is necessary for people to pass securely and this means exchanging mutual assistance. Debrief for giving and receiving help. Compare with the previous activity. Discuss trust, support, and cooperation. Did people follow through on the behaviors they stood for at the start?

Variations: Require everyone to start over for more difficulty. Allow people to talk for greater ease.

47 Restructuring the Company

PROPS: 1   **TIME:** 10-30   **ALIAS:** Magic Carpet, FSIII-37
MOVE: 2   **SIZE:** 5-20   **ORIGIN:** Unknown

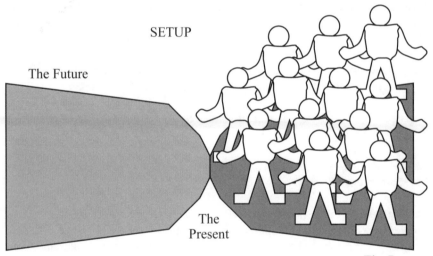

You are living in the past of this organization (standing on this side of the tarp). Without abandoning it (don't step off), please restructure your organization into the future (turn the tarp over and stand on its other side). Should you accidentally leave the organization during the restructuring (allow a small part of your body to touch ground), your group will have to return to the past and try again (start over from the beginning). Any questions?

Action: Group stands on a plastic tarp and turns it over to stand on the other side without anyone stepping off.

Intent: Cooperation, communication, trust, leadership, and problem solving.

Note: Tarp size is critical in this activity (if unsure about sizes, test this activity with a facilitator group first).

Equipment: A plastic tarp (sized so that the entire group could just crowd onto one half of its fully opened area).

Setup: Present the group with the tarp and ask them to write their hopes and dreams for the future of their organization on one side. Once they have done this, ask them to turn the tarp over and write down all the things they have not liked about the organization in the past. Then, when finished, have the group stand on the tarp.

Task: To turn the tarp over and stand on the other side without stepping off.

Constraints: If just one person happens to touch ground outside the tarp, everyone must start over again.

Safety: Spot anyone who gets lifted off the ground (perhaps piggyback style). Otherwise, restrict people from lifting in this activity. Prepare for the action to occur in a wide open space well away from any obstacles.

Facilitation: The group usually crowds into one half of the tarp and then flips it over wave curl or bow tie style and then begins stepping over to the other side, before straightening up the rest of the vacated half. Discuss what abandoning the organization means. Debrief for the teamwork skills that each person contributed that led to successful flipping the tarp and how those real skills will prove useful in actually restructuring the organization.

Variations: Conduct this nonverbally for greater difficulty. Choose larger tarp sizes for greater ease.

48   **Corporate Mergers**

PROPS: 1 **TIME:** 20-40 **ALIAS:** Shrinking Circles, QS-172
MOVE: 2 **SIZE:** 10-40 **ORIGIN:** Steve Butler

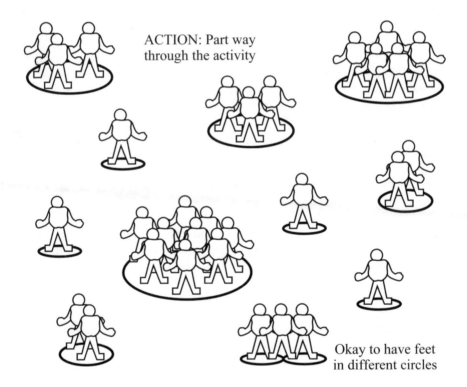

ACTION: Part way through the activity

Okay to have feet in different circles

You are all employed by a series of related companies (standing in these circles). In a moment, you will hear about a merger between some of these companies (a circle will be removed) and all of you will need to find new employment with another related company (everyone must go to a remaining circle). You are all looking for full time employment (everyone's feet must be entirely inside a circle), and once everyone is gainfully employed (all feet inside circles), we will continue with our merging process. Any questions?... MERGER!

Action: People must stand inside circles, but as they switch to a new circle, the number of circles decrease.

Intent: Creative thinking, competition versus cooperation, sharing resources, and collaboration.

Note: As people switch circles, swiftly take one away (remove smaller ones first and leave larger ones for later).

Equipment: A number of different sized circles of rope or cord (start with fewer circles than half the people).

Setup: Spread the rope circles out around the area (make sure there is about 10' or more between circles) and invite people to stand inside them (some circles may contain one person, while others will hold several people).

Task: To keep everyone's feet inside a circle. The activity will not progress unless all feet are inside a circle.

Constraints: You cannot move any circles. You cannot prevent the facilitator from removing any circles.

Safety: Practice and encourage shuffling (where the feet maintain contact with the ground) instead of walking. If people begin to lift one another off the ground, simply explain that the elevated person's feet are not in the circle.

Facilitation: The solution to this problem is to sit or lie on the ground and allow only feet in the circle. However, many people approach this like musical chairs not wishing to be the one left out and without a job. This can lead to a rush for survival at the expense of others. Discuss this concern and how survival, selfishness, selflessness, and sharing occurred and were received. Debrief for competition versus cooperation and creativity.

Variations: Allow people to move or touch the circles (perhaps they will retie a larger circle from several smaller ones). Require only one foot on the ground (the other can get raised up, rather than rested outside the circle).

49   Group Golf

PROPS: 3   **TIME:** 120-240   **ALIAS:** Executive Marbles, EM-68
MOVE: 2   **SIZE:**   4-16   **ORIGIN:** Sam Sikes, The Cherokee

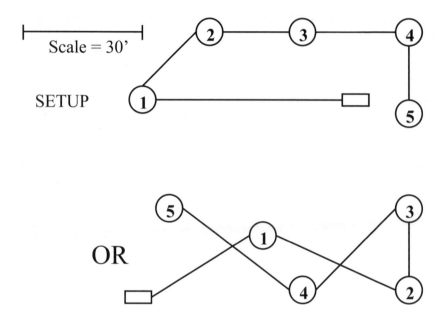

The goal of this activity is for one subgroup member to complete the course (with the support of fellow members and despite the strategy of the other subgroup) using four kinds of shots. 1 = A SHOT: Place your feet together on the spot where your ball last landed. Without supporting yourself by touching any other body part to anything, throw over or underhand (you must let go of the ball). If your ball doesn't hit another ball or go into a hole, it simply stays where it stops rolling. 2 = ANOTHER SHOT: If your ball hits another ball directly on the fly (not rolling), or after a single bounce (not two or more), then you get an extra shot. 3 = COMPLETED SHOT: If your ball is placed or rolls into a hole when you are shooting, then you pick up your ball and wait for your next turn to shoot from this hole. If someone knocks your ball in a hole for you, this does not count (place your ball beside the hole and take a Completed Shot later). 4 = WINNING SHOT: If you have made 8 Completed Shots in the correct sequence of holes (1-2-3-4-5-4-3-2), then your 9th Completed Shot (into No.1) wins the game for your subgroup. Here is a written summary of these four kinds of shots for your subgroup to refer to during play. Any questions? We'll tee off from here, subgroups will alternate turns and members will go in order of ball numbers: 1,9,2,10,3,11...

Action: A combination of golf, croquet, snooker, and bocce played with two equal sized subgroups of 2-8 players.

Intent: Teamwork, conflict, competition, communication, cooperation, leadership, planning, and strategy.

Note: This is one competitive activity that has many non-competitive lessons.

Equipment: Five flags to mark holes and one billiard ball per person for outdoor play (indoors: use tape to mark the holes and substitute coin-filled tennis balls).

Setup: Design and layout the course. Although the shape of a 7 or L is traditional, any shape will do and often criss-crossing fairways (see diagram) provides for more potential conflict and interesting strategies. Make the holes by depressing a ball into soft ground and plant a flag nearby. Pick subgroups by having people choose a ball from a cloth bag to determine their memberships (stripes versus solids). Select a starting place (first tee) and assemble the subgroups there to explain and demonstrate the rules of play. Provide a written summary for them.

Task: For at least one subgroup member to complete all nine holes of the obstacle-rich course, in the correct sequence (1-2-3-4-5-4-3-2-1), according to the rules of play, and perhaps by repeatedly knocking others' balls around.

Constraints: In this game, one can repeatedly hit another ball and get unlimited Another Shots until missing or completing a shot. This is part of the excitement and variability, but can result in prolonged time spent watching. To make the game move faster, and to be less one sided, consider limiting the number of Another Shots that may be taken by players during a turn. If falling during a shot, one must release the ball before touching the ground or lose your turn.

Safety: Make sure people know when a Shot is coming their way (so they won't need to wear helmets). The rule of standing with feet together and not supporting oneself can make balance difficult: bend this rule as needed. Remove obstacles, especially before someone slam dunks their Completed Shot or dives in an effort to hit other balls and get Another Shot.

Facilitation: Take frequent breaks as needed to facilitate the group process. Discuss initial reactions to subgroup selection, strategy planning, winning or losing, competition, and the gamut of teamwork learning outcomes.

Variations: Be prepared for subgroups to choose complex strategies of offense and defense and break the rules. Vary the number of subgroups, members, etc.

50   Saving Stranded Motorists

PROPS: 3   **TIME:** 30-60   **ALIAS:** Screen Retrieval, GWA-71
MOVE: 2   **SIZE:** 5-10   **ORIGIN:** British Facilitators via S.P.

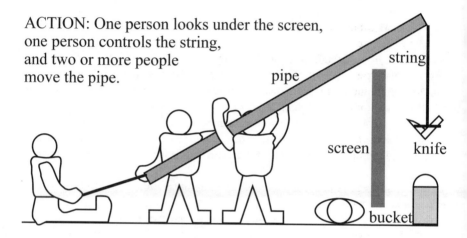

ACTION: One person looks under the screen, one person controls the string, and two or more people move the pipe.

Your auto club call center typically responds to a stranded motorist in under 20 minutes by sending out a tow truck and drivers supported by all your staff and available databases. In this activity, an auto club member (bucket) is stranded in an unknown location (somewhere on the other side of this screen) and your task has three parts. First, find the best tow truck and drivers from your available database (make a retrieval device from these resources and choose who will operate it). Second, dispatch the tow truck and drivers to the general area (operate the device from this side of the screen only, without a person or resource touching the screen). Third, specifically locate and then rescue the motorist (retrieve the bucket) with direction from one call center agent who is currently on the phone with that motorist (a person lying on the floor and looking under the screen, not around or over it). If the tow truck or drivers are involved with an accident on the way to rescue the auto club member, they will be recalled and a similar tow truck with new drivers will be dispatched (if a person or the retrieval device touches the screen at any time, then the device will be returned to this side of the screen and new people will be chosen to operate it). This should be achieved in less than your established quality criterion of 20 minutes. Any questions?

Action: Group creates a device that lets them retrieve a partially visible bucket from behind a screened off area.

Intent: Communication, cooperation, coordination, problem solving, and leadership.

Note: To prevent silhouetted solutions, the tarp used in this activity must not be translucent (even when back lit).

Equipment: A bucket, pocket knife (hinged type), ball of string, 10' long PVC pipe, and opaque 8'x20' tarp.

Setup: Hang the tarp vertically as an 8' high screen with a 6" gap between the screen bottom and the ground. Place the bucket on one side of the screen (6" from it) and the rest of equipment on the other side with the group.

Task: To create a device with the allocated resources to retrieve an unseen bucket from behind an opaque screen.

Constraints: If people or resources touch the screen, swap people and start over. Only look under the screen.

Safety: People will want to get on one another's backs or shoulders to look over the top of the screen. This may be unsafe (and creates too simple a solution). Find a way to restrict against this and request people stay down on the ground.

Facilitation: The key is to see the knife as a hook, rather than a cutting tool. It can be tied in the partially open position and dangled from the string (which runs through the pipe), so the whole system can be used as a crane to hook the bucket. Another revelation is to have the person looking beneath the screen also control the string. Debrief for communication, cooperation, leadership, and creative thinking associated with these two realizations.

Variations: The task gets easier and physically riskier, if there is no gap beneath the screen, and one person sits on the shoulders of another, looking over the screen and maneuvering the retrieval device. To make the task more difficult, fill the bucket with water and tape off a very tight work space that the group must stay within.

51   Removing Waste Products

PROPS: 3   **TIME:** 30-60   **ALIAS:** The Grabber, NEW
MOVE: 1   **SIZE:** 5-15   **ORIGIN:** German Facilitators, S.P.

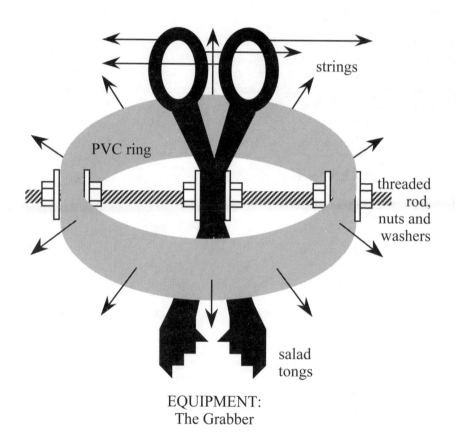

strings

PVC ring

threaded
rod,
nuts and
washers

salad
tongs

EQUIPMENT:
The Grabber

In this activity, you will use this collection device to remove all waste products (objects) without entering the toxic tank (marked area) before they accumulate to threatening proportions (20 minutes).   If any waste product destabilizes (mousetrap set off), the volume of waste products increases (more objects added). Any questions?

Action: Group maneuvers a collection device to pick up and remove a variety of objects.

Intent: Cooperation, coordination, communication, trust, leadership, and decision making.

Note: The collection device can be premade by the facilitator using: fourteen 20' lengths of string; a PVC ring; a threaded rod with several nuts and washers; and a hinged pair of plastic or wooden salad tongs. As shown in the diagram, drill through the center of the salad tongs and PVC ring. Suspend the salad tongs in the middle of the PVC ring using the threaded rod, nuts, and washers. Drill additional holes in the PVC ring and attach the ten strings. Attach the other four strings to the grips of the salad tongs, two per grip as shown in the diagram opposite.

Equipment: One collection device (as above) and a variety of objects (bean bags, balls, and one mousetrap).

Setup: Spread the objects (including the mousetrap) around inside a taped boundary area and lay the collection device beside them with the strings spread out so that the string ends reach outside the taped boundaries. Assemble the group around the area.

Task: To clear a boundary area of all objects within a time limit, by using the device to collect and remove them.

Constraints: Do not enter the taped area or touch objects. If a mousetrap is set off in an attempt to move it, extra objects get added into the taped area as a penalty.

Safety: Caution that people may get pulled off balance by others pulling too hard on strings across from them.

Facilitation: Picking up objects is the hardest action to synchronize. Debrief for cooperation and coordination.

Variations: People can figure out how to make their own device, when given the disassembled pieces above. Attach a drawing marker to the PVC ring and have the group sketch their company logo or write a word like TEAM on a large piece of paper. Add blindfolds and a sighted supervisor to make the task extremely difficult.

52   **Winning Back Customers**

PROPS: 3   **TIME:** 30-60   **ALIAS:** Tree Retrieval, BBA-110
MOVE: 3   **SIZE:** 5-15   **ORIGIN:** Karl Rohnke

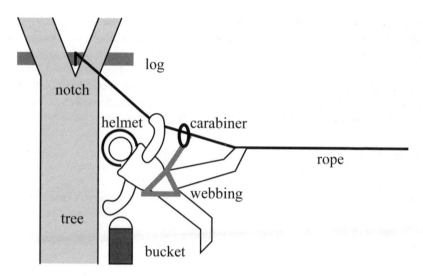

ACTION: Retriever supported by the group

Disappointed with poor human service and frustrated with technology, a cluster of customers (bucket of water) are about to choose your competitor in the next 20 minutes. Using your technology (equipment issued to you), win back those customers (retrieve the bucket) from your competitor's sphere of influence (marked off area that you are not allowed to set foot within). Avoid further customer loss (water spillage) by caring for all of them with your best human contact and not letting technology interfere (only people may touch the bucket and not any equipment), otherwise the amount of lost customers will grow (water will be increased). Any questions?

Action: While the group holds a rope tight, one person hangs from it by a harness and retrieves a water bucket.

Intent: Problem solving, cooperation, communication, risk taking, support, and trust.

Note: This activity requires a big tree with a tight notch between two strong branches. This location will need to bear the weight of a person, so if facilitators are not capable of choosing a safe location, find experts to assist.

Equipment: A bucket of water, two 100' climbing ropes, 20' of climbing webbing, a locking carabiner, and a 3' long section of a 3" diameter (or greater) log. A helmet for the retriever is a strongly recommended option here.

Setup: Find a tree with a notch as described above that is about 10-20' above very soft ground. Lay the bucket of water close to the base of the tree and mark a 30' diameter circle around the tree base and bucket using one of the 100' ropes. Give the other 100' rope, log, webbing, and carabiner to the people, who are outside this circle.

Task: To get the bucket of water out of the circle before time runs out and without stepping into the circle.

Constraints: Resources must not touch the bucket, but people may touch it. Stepping inside the circle, spilling the water, or touching the bucket with any piece of equipment all cause more water to be added to the bucket.

Safety: Double check that the method used to attach the retriever to the rope, the rope to the log, and the log to the tree is secure and will not permit a fall. Double check that the harness made from webbing will not impede breathing or circulation for the retriever.

Facilitation: Groups commonly tie the rope to the log and toss it between the notch, pulling back to hold it in place. Then, they fashion a harness for the retriever from the webbing, clip it to the rope with the carabiner, and pull back with all their weight to lift the retriever off the ground. Debrief for planning, trust, support, risk taking, and communication. Discuss giving technological service versus using technology to help people serve people.

Variations: Consider blindfolding group members for added difficulty. Allow other trees to be used for anchors or additional support, but be sure to warn people about not damaging trees by pulling ropes across their bark.

53   **Accessing Archived Data**

PROPS: 3   **TIME:** 30-90   **ALIAS:** Amazon, SB-137
MOVE: 3   **SIZE:** 5-15   **ORIGIN:** Project Adventure

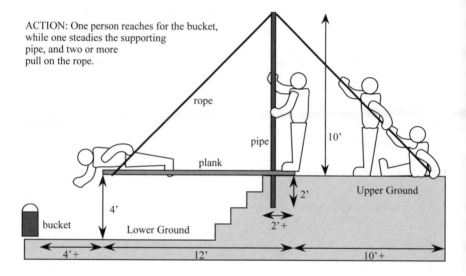

ACTION: One person reaches for the bucket, while one steadies the supporting pipe, and two or more pull on the rope.

rope

pipe

plank

10'

2'

Upper Ground

4'

bucket   Lower Ground

2' +

4' +   12'   10' +

A critical data set (bucket) must be retrieved from the archives (lower ground) in 20 minutes. Available resources (items on higher ground) may be used for data access only, but may damage all data if used for retrieval (bucket moves further away, if any resource touches the bucket or any person or resource touches lower ground).

Action: Through a cantilevered bridge system, one person attempts to retrieve a bucket while the group supports.

Intent: Problem solving, cooperation, communication, risk taking, support, and trust.

Note: Find an embankment or staircase where the elevation difference between upper and lower ground is about 4'. Soft ground surrounding helps lessen possible falls and allows a steel pipe to be anchored 2' in the ground.

Equipment: A 12' long 2"x8" plank, a 12' long 2" diameter steel pipe, a bucket, and 30' of climbing rope.

Setup: Drill a 2" wide hole in the plank about 1' from one end (the pipe must fit through here). Drill a 1" hole about 6" from the other end (the rope may be tied here). Put the assembly together (as shown in the diagram) to test it first. The 12' plank extends horizontally about 10' into the air, with about 2' of contact with the ground. The 12' pipe goes vertically through the hole in the plank and 2' into the ground. The rope is tied to the far end of the plank, goes over the top of the pipe (may be tied here) and down to the anchoring group. Place the bucket about 4' farther away from the plank. Then disassemble everything else and leave all these items on high ground.

Task: To retrieve the bucket without touching ground and by using resources for access only and not retrieval.

Constraints: Penalty when resources touch the bucket, and when people or resources touch the lower ground.

Safety: Remind the retrieving person not to place arms or legs underneath the plank, in case they get dropped.

Facilitation: Debrief for risk taking, support, trust, and communication. Discuss miscommunications and supporting roles.

Variations: Add a stick for easier retrieval of the bucket. Add water or weight to the bucket for more difficulty.

54   **Building a Network**

PROPS: 2   **TIME:** 30-90   **ALIAS:** Ravine, GWA-64
MOVE: 3   **SIZE:** 5-10   **ORIGIN:** British Facilitators via S.P.

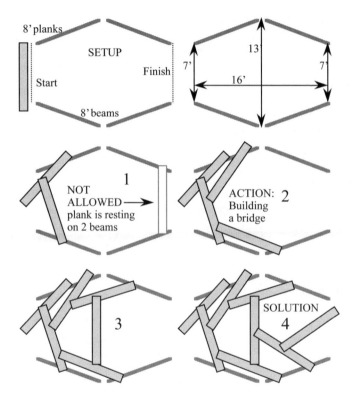

Your task is two fold: build a network and test it. First, create a continuous network by linking a series of fiber optic cables to one another (planks must contact other planks), across this organizational void (area in between the beams), using only one linkage with the supporting infrastructure per cable (each plank can only rest once on a beam). The first and last cable should link the two servers though the network (the first and last plank must connect over the start and finish lines respectively). Second, test the completed network by sending a continuous data stream (line of people maintaining constant contact with one another) between the two servers. If any cable or data gets lost in the void, then the cable will need replacing and all the data will need to be transferred again (planks touching the ground go back to the start, a person touching sends everyone back). Any questions?

Action: To walk over an open area, people create a bridge of planks resting on widely separated support beams.

Intent: Problem solving, planning, helping behaviors, trust, support, cooperation, and communication.

Note: The original one of these was built over a mud creek, but this activity is best conducted on flat soft ground.

Equipment: Eight 8' planks (2"x8"), four 8' beams (4"x4"), and rope or tape to mark start and finish lines.

Setup: The 4 beams are laid out in a hexagon pattern as diagrammed. The 8 planks and people gather at the start.

Task: To build a bridge by resting planks on beams and to have the group cross over while maintaining contact.

Constraints: Each plank may only rest on one beam. First and last planks must cross over the start and finish lines respectively. All planks must touch another plank and people must remain connected when they cross over.

Safety: Caution people not to rush across as this may collapse the planks and cause someone to trip and fall.

Facilitation: Other than determining the best plank pattern, the other key to success is helping behaviors. Ask for examples of how help was offered or requested and tie these examples back to trust and support in the group.

Variations: Ask them to take all the planks with them to the other side. This requires that they disassemble and reassemble the bridge in reversed configuration. Provide more planks or closer beams for a much easier task.

55   Computer Disinfectant

PROPS: 2   **TIME:** 30-60   **ALIAS:** Nuclear Reactor, BM-151
MOVE: 2   **SIZE:** 10-20   **ORIGIN:** Mike Gass & Simon Priest

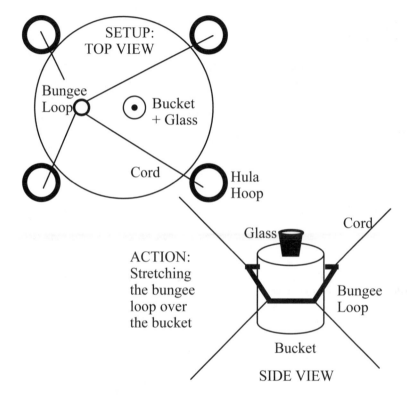

Your company's computer server (circle) contains a piece of software (bucket) that has been infected with a virus (glass of water). Your task is to remove the virus and the infected software (get both cup and bucket out of the circle) without crashing the server (don't spill the water in or out of the circle) and before the deadline of 30 minutes expires. You have the resources (bungee cord and rope) to write a disinfectant subroutine (build a lifting tool). However, this can only be constructed and operated by pairs of collaborating workers protected from electromagnetic discharge (blindfolded and gloved) while sitting at their terminals (standing in hula hoops). Networking is provided by four supervisors and a coordinating leader. No one may enter the server or touch the software or virus. Each infraction accelerates the system toward a crash (lose 1 minute of time). Any questions?

Action: Group constructs a device to lift and move an inverted bucket without spilling the glass of water on top.

Intent: Teamwork, cooperation, communication, trust, leadership, problem solving, and systems thinking.

Note: The lifting device may be uniquely created by each group or can be premade by facilitators to save time.

Equipment: Pickle bucket, plastic glass, supply of water (or beans for indoors), 8 blindfolds, 4 hula hoops, a single 3' piece of bungee cord, four 20' lengths of cord, a rope or tape to mark boundaries, and 4 pairs of gloves.

Setup: Mark out a 20' circle with tape or rope. Place the pickle bucket upside down in the middle with a glass of water on top. Equally space hula hoops around the perimeter of the circle (as in the diagram). Appoint (or have the group choose) a leader and 4 supervisors. Check that the remainder won't mind wearing blindfolds (if they do, they can observe). If the facilitator chooses to make the device (instead of letting the group), one design is to tie the ends of the bungee cord into a tiny tight loop (large enough to fit over the bucket when stretched, but small enough to fit snugly around the bucket when relaxed). Lastly, tie the ends of the four cords to this bungee loop.

Task: To get the pickle bucket and glass of water out of the circle without spilling water or breaking any rules.

Constraints: Can't touch anything except the cord and must be wearing a blindfold and gloves when doing this. Can't enter the circle. Workers must stay within their hula hoops. Consequences are loss of time from deadline.

Safety: The thin cord can bite into unprotected hands, supply gloves or encourage people to wrap cord around their waists and pull with their legs and not arms. Ask the group to attend to the safety of blindfolded members.

Facilitation: Discuss feelings of empathy for others (especially if usual work roles were reversed) and treatment of blindfolded people. Otherwise, this is a rich exercise for communication issues and common teamwork topics.

Variations: The task is typically conducted by the blindfolded workers pulling on the end of the cords, while getting direction from the supervisors and coordination from a leader. Groups may find unexpected alternatives. A very difficult version has the bucket floating in a swimming pool with everyone pulling from the edge.

56   **Obtaining Raw Materials**

PROPS: 2   **TIME:**   20-40   **ALIAS:**   Giant Lizard Egg, ZG-50
MOVE: 2   **SIZE:**   5-10   **ORIGIN:** Sam Sikes, Steve Balsters

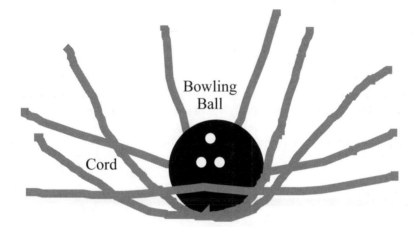

Bowling Ball

Cord

ONE SOLUTION

These (indicate the bowling balls) represent raw materials that you are interested in getting from your supplier (behind start line) to your manufacturing plant (behind finish line). Unfortunately, these materials are both delicate and dangerous: they require great care and special handling to transport. You have been supplied with these devices (cord) and must construct a way to transport the materials according to these criteria. First, the materials are explosive to the touch. Second, they are intensely illuminating and so anyone within three feet of them must be using protective eyewear (blindfolds). Third, any hazardous spill of the materials (show ball hitting the ground) will blind anyone not wearing protective eyewear (and so people may need to swap roles). Fourth, clean up of the spill will cost one team member to be injured (becomes an observer), but the rest of your group will need to return to the supplier to begin again with a new shipment of raw materials. Fifth, you may choose to redesign your transport system at any time or place, as long as you do not cause a toxic spill. Last, one delivery of raw materials must be at the manufacturing plant before the deadline of 20 minutes from now. Any questions?

Action: Group constructs a cradle from cord to carry a bowling ball over an obstacle course.

Intent: Teamwork, cooperation, communication, trust, problem solving, leadership, planning, and execution.

Note: The obstacles could be as simple as uneven ground or other items could be added for more difficulty.

Equipment: Several large and heavy bowling balls, a dozen pieces of 6' cord, and tape or rope (other obstacles).

Setup: Using the tape or rope, mark out a starting and finishing area (preferably with uneven ground in between the two places). Place one bowling ball behind the start line and randomly scatter the short pieces of cord nearby.

Task: Safely get the raw materials (ball) from supplier (start) to manufacturing (finish) within the set time limit.

Constraints: Don't touch the ball. Wear blindfolds when transporting. Each time ball gets dropped, people swap blindfolded roles, everyone starts over, and the group loses one member to observe performance.

Safety: Remind people to take care by keeping their hands and feet out of danger should the material be dropped.

Facilitation: Discuss the usual team lessons related to problem solving, planning, execution, and especially communication. If observers are created by ball drops, be sure to get their input during the debrief session.

Variations: A minimum of 3 or 4 pieces of cord are necessary to transport a bowling ball. Therefore, challenge the group to accomplish this task again, but differently: with fewer hands and/or in less time. Consider adding preset mousetraps or other items from the minefield experience (#37) to the list of obstacles en route. Give the obstacles relevant names or descriptions that would relate to the normal transport of potentially hazardous toxins.

57   **Disseminating Supplies**

PROPS: 3   **TIME:** 20-40   **ALIAS:** Toxic Waste, QS-178
MOVE: 2   **SIZE:** 5-10   **ORIGIN:** Project Adventure

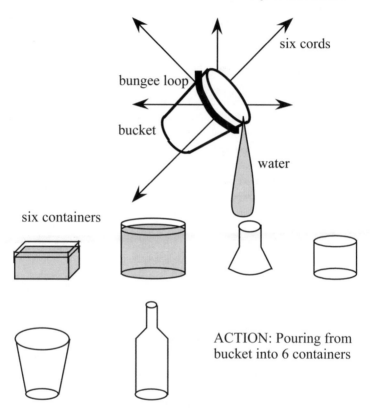

six cords

bungee loop

bucket

water

six containers

ACTION: Pouring from
bucket into 6 containers

In the next 20 minutes, you need to disseminate your raw materials (water) from this distribution facility (bucket) to your factories by filling (to a level of 1" or less below the rim) these six containers. This raw product is kept stable in liquid nitrogen and so the distribution facility and six containers cannot be touched directly (start over if anyone touches a bucket or container). Instead, you will construct a transfer device from these resources (bungee cord and six cords) and everyone will use it to handle the materials with great care. You must maintain constant contact with the transfer device (start over if you break contact with the cords), but cannot get within 10' of the liquid nitrogen (so hold the ends of the cords). Spillage of raw materials requires a complete cleanup: so the most recently filled container will be emptied, before you continue on. Any questions?

Action: Group distributes water from one bucket into several containers using a collar attachment only.

Intent: Communication, cooperation, coordination, planning, problem solving, and leadership.

Note: If working indoors, substitute beans for water. Gloves are optional for this activity.

Equipment: A bucket of water, six smaller containers of various sizes, 3' of bungee cord, and six 10' cords.

Setup: Put the water bucket, six containers, bungee cord, and six cords on the ground. Assemble the group.

Task: To fill all containers (to a level within 1" from the rim) without spilling any water and before time runs out.

Constraints: Penalty for spillage means emptying one already filled container. Everyone must maintain contact with the cords at all times. Start over if anyone touches the bucket or a container, and if anyone lets go of a cord.

Safety: If cord bites into unprotected hands, provide gloves. Watch out for potentially slippery floors.

Facilitation: The group typically ties a loop of bungee cord and attaches all six cords to it. They pull together on the six cords to stretch the bungee loop over the bucket and then relax the bungee to grip the bucket. Often the loop is not adjusted tightly enough to handle the weight of a full bucket, so water may be spilled at the start. The most difficult transfer step is pouring water from the bucket into a container. This necessitates some people getting as low as they can, while others get as high as possible. If this step is troublesome, allow people to hold the cords anywhere. Debrief for creativity, assumptions, and planning. Discuss leadership and communication.

Variations: For added difficulty, put the six containers in six designated areas that no one is allowed to enter and at different heights or close to obstacles.

58   Conveyer Systems

PROPS: 3   **TIME:** 30-60   **ALIAS:** Bull Rings, TT-79
MOVE: 2   **SIZE:** 5-15   **ORIGIN:** American Facilitators, J.C.

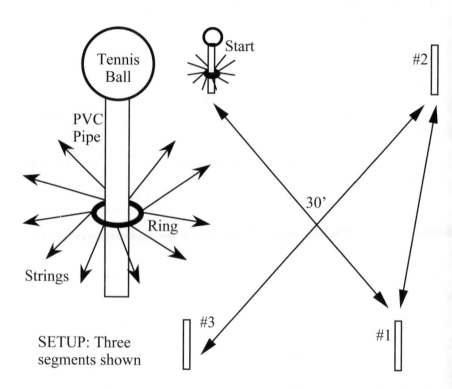

SETUP: Three
segments shown

In your factory, you have three manufacturing processes: reflection; integration; and continuation. The start and finish of each process is marked by these standards (pipes). Your task is to transport the product (ball) through these three processes using this conveyer system (ring) operated only by these controls (strings). The first process is reflection, where conditions are perfect (no constraints). The second process is integration, where conditions are so noisy you can't hear (no speaking). The third process is continuation, where conditions are so bright that you can't see (keep your eyes closed), but you may select one sighted individual to help you work. The sequence must be finished within 20 minutes. If you drop any product off the conveyer (drop a ball), or interfere with product, process or conveyer (don't touch the ball, ring, or pipes), just start over from the beginning with a new product. Any questions?

Action: The group carries a ball on a ring held by multiple strings, from resting pipe to resting pipe.

Intent: Communication, leadership, planning, problem solving, and trust.

Note: Although three segments are mentioned here, feel free to layout additional ones and design these as needed for the manufacturer.

Equipment: Ten 10' string lengths, four 1" diameter 4' long PVC pipes, one 2" diameter ring, and 3" diameter balls (tennis balls seem to work better than golf balls).

Setup: Stand the PVC pipes vertically with about 1' anchored in the ground and separate them by about 30' each. Tie the ten pieces of string to the ring and then slip the ring over one pipe. Let the ring rest on the ground, with the strings spread out widely. Place one ball atop that standing pipe (keep the others) and gather the group.

Task: To complete three legs of a journey by carrying a ball among four resting pipes without dropping it.

Constraints: No talking for everyone on the second leg and all but one without sight on the third. Start over if you drop the ball. Hold only the strings. Don't touch the ball, ring, or pipes, otherwise you start over again.

Safety: Be prepared to halt the action if anyone is about to bump into something, especially during the third and final leg.

Facilitation: Debrief for communication. Discuss the number of dropped balls and what this depicts at work.

Variations: Provide blindfolds for those who have difficulty keeping their eyes closed. Add additional legs of the journey with other constraints: obstacles, uneven ground, narrow spaces, hidden or angled pipes, ankles tied together, etc. Vary the size of the balls and rings to alter the challenge. Substitute large ice cubes for balls.

59   **Goods to the Warehouse**

PROPS: 2   **TIME:** 20-40   **ALIAS:** Waterfall, EM-198
MOVE: 2   **SIZE:**   2-10   **ORIGIN:** Joel Cryer & Tim Reed

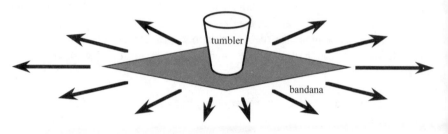

ACTION: People pull on the edges of
the bandana to keep the tumbler level

You are working with finished products (water or beans) in their shipping containers (plastic tumbler) and you are interested in getting the goods from manufacturing (start line) to the warehouse (finish line) without encountering any problems (obstacles) which may delay or prevent a successful on time delivery of 20 minutes. Your transportation device is this forklift pallet (bandana) and your team will work the forklift (combined hands). Once your forklift has contacted the pallet, you must maintain contact until the warehouse is reached. The pallet must remain under tension and be kept below the lip of the container at all times. Loss of product (water spillage) requires that the container be returned to the warehouse to be refilled and two team members will survive injuries from the industrial accident (a pair will temporarily have their ankles or wrists tied together three-legged race style). Once the pallet is ready and the forklift is working, I'll place a full container on board. Any questions?

Action: Carrying a tumbler of water atop a tension stretched bandana through obstacles without spilling a drop.

Intent: Teamwork, cooperation, communication, trust, leadership, problem solving, planning, and execution.

Note: If indoors, fill the tumbler with beans instead of water. Add creative obstacles as in activity #56. Make sure the tumbler is not made from glass.

Equipment: One bandana and plastic tumbler (full of water or beans) per group, tape or rope (and obstacles).

Setup: Mark out boundaries, start and finish lines with the tape or rope. Arrange obstacles in between the start and finish or select a naturally challenging route. Pass out a bandana and a filled plastic tumbler to each group.

Task: Carry the water (or beans) without spilling any through obstacles from manufacturing to the warehouse.

Constraints: Always hold on to the bandana by the edge (can't role it up). The bandana must remain flat and taught beneath the tumbler (can't cover or secure the tumbler in any way). Start over at the beginning for any spillage and two people get their ankles or wrists tied together (for safety, the facilitator chooses who).

Safety: People tend to fixate on the water and not pay attention to where they place their feet. Spot for missteps.

Facilitation: Discuss the usual team lessons related to problem solving, trust, cooperation, and communication.

Variations: Before using the bandana, participants can draw on it and write down their goals, fears, anticipated behaviors, and new learning. Begin and end with the bandana and tumbler on the ground. Allow the group to choose their level of risk and decide how full the tumbler will be. Encourage many trips in order to actually fill a bucket with several tumblers of water or beans, this makes for more speed and efficiency risks.

60   **Delivering to Market**

PROPS: 3   **TIME:** 30-60   **ALIAS:** Communication, ZG-84
MOVE: 1   **SIZE:** 5-10   **ORIGIN:** Sam Sikes and others

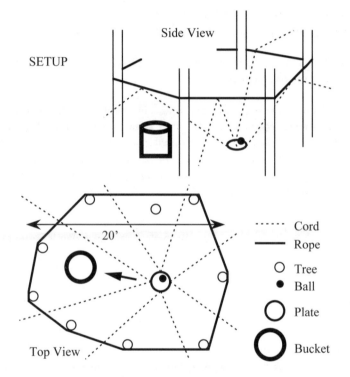

You are delivering your newest product (indicate the ball) to market (the bucket), using a sophisticated containerized system (flat plate), operated like so (demonstrate using only one hand and pulling only one cord). Unfortunately, this complex system cannot be operated with both your hands on the same set of controls (you must have hands on different cords). This product is highly unstable. If it is dropped from its container and not retrieved by the container within 60 seconds, then two injured transport workers will need to be replaced (the two people who are farthest away and closest to the ball must exchange their roles and the activity starts over with the facilitator replacing the ball). Due to the volatility of this product, no one should touch anything within this safety perimeter (rope boundary). Crossing this boundary with any part of your body brings instant blindness (hold up a blindfold) the first time and certain death a second time (that person becomes an observer). Any questions?

Action: By manipulating strings attached to a flat plate holding a ball, the group deposits the ball into a bucket.

Intent: Teamwork, cooperation, communication, trust, problem solving, leadership, planning, and execution.

Note: If a circle of trees is not available, purchase or build a specialized structure out of PVC piping.

Equipment: Plastic plate, ball, bucket, eight 20' pieces of cord, one 100' rope, blindfolds, and a circle of trees.

Setup: Find a circle of trees around an open space (or create one using poles or furniture). Tie the rope around that circle under tension (as in the diagram, so it is tight enough to support the weight of the other equipment) and about 3' off the ground. Drill eight holes through the plastic plate at places near its edge and thread the cords freely through these holes. Next, place the bucket and the plate on the ground inside the circle of rope with all eight cords radiating away from the plate, but draped over the tight rope. Lastly, put the ball atop the flat plate.

Task: To get the ball into the bucket without dropping it and only by manipulating the cords attached to the plate.

Constraints: Do not touch the plate, ball, or bucket and stay completely out of the circle (no hands past the rope) or suffer the consequences. You may use two hands per cord (just not the same pair of hands) and you may use both your hands (just not on the same cord). If a ball gets dropped, you have 1 minute to scoop it up with the plate (otherwise, the two people who are closest to and farthest from its final resting spot must change places with one another).

Safety: Make sure the surrounding area is free of dangers.

Facilitation: Discuss the effect that independent efforts have on a group goal.

Variations: Fasten rings to the encircling rope and pass the cords through these rings, thereby requiring a fixed point of operation. Experiment with different types of balls (big/small, heavy/light). Coat the underside of the plate with sticky glue, spread real or play money about the circle, and have the group pick up as much profit as then can. For greater difficulty, try this with more blindfolds and directions from one or more sighted members.

61   Sampling Public Opinion

PROPS: 4   **TIME:** 30-60   **ALIAS:** Under the Bridge, GWA-74
MOVE: 2   **SIZE:** 5-10   **ORIGIN:** British Facilitators via S.P.

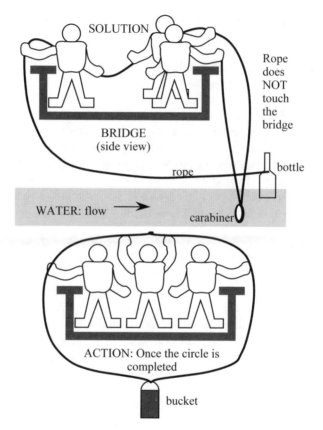

Your task is to sample the public's opinion about your most recent ad campaign
(obtain a water sample) and to pass their opinions around the office twice for
co-worker's comments (make two circuits under and over this bridge). You
must remain in your office at all times, but always near the public (stay on the
bridge and over the water). Only use your sampling equipment outside the office
(equipment can't touch the bridge, but people can) and conduct your sampling
without directly engaging the public (people can't touch the water, but equipment
can). If equipment is used inside the office or you get too closely involved with
sampling (equipment touches the bridge or you touch the water), then the sample
will need to be retaken (everything starts over). Any questions?

Action: To obtain a water sample from a bridge and then to pass that sample over and under the bridge twice.

Intent: Problem solving, creativity, planning, communication, cooperation, trust, and leadership.

Note: This activity needs a safe sturdy bridge over water (moving rivers have advantages over stationary lakes).

Equipment: One rope (length is four times the distance from bridge to water), a bucket, a bottle and a carabiner.

Setup: Place all the equipment on the bridge and assemble the group near the center section of the bridge.

Task: To obtain a water sample and to pass it over and under the bridge twice, without violating any restrictions.

Constraints: You must stay on the bridge section that is over water (can't leave the bridge or stand over land). Equipment must not touch the bridge, but may touch the water. No tying off rope and then throwing it around. People should not touch the water, but may touch the bridge. Start over from the beginning for any infractions.

Safety: Discourage leaning over the bridge so far as to fall in. Consider PFD's for non-swimmers or ask everyone to wear one.

Facilitation: One solution involves getting the rope to encircle the bridge. Simply throwing it over or under won't work because the resources can't touch the bridge. Using the carabiner as a weight, a looped section of the rope can be lowered into the water on the downstream side of the bridge by two people, while the other end can be tied to the bottle or bucket as a float and be put in the upstream side by one person. When the float crosses above the weight, the looped rope is raised to make a circle. Debrief for problem solving and creative thinking.

Variations: Allow equipment to touch the bridge for an easier solution. For greater difficulty, request circuits be completed within set time limits. Request multiple water samples by using both the bottle and the bucket together.

62   **Plugging Leaks with P.R.**

PROPS: 2   **TIME:** 20-40   **ALIAS:** Punctured Drum, SB-125
MOVE: 2   **SIZE:** 10-20   **ORIGIN:** Classic

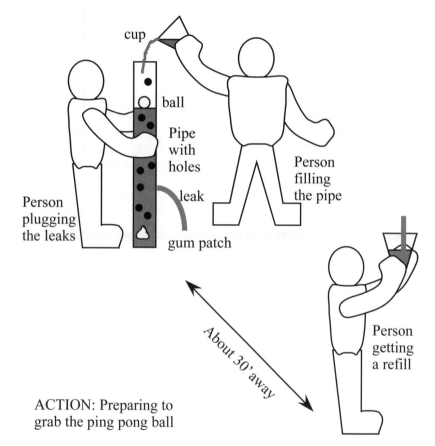

cup

ball

Pipe
with
holes

leak

Person
plugging
the leaks

gum patch

Person
filling
the pipe

About 30' away

Person
getting
a refill

ACTION: Preparing to
grab the ping pong ball

You have encountered a crisis in your motionless organization (fixed pipe) and have endured a great deal of bad press (ping pong ball) from the media due to abundant information leaks (holes in the pipe). Your task in public relations is to erase the bad press (remove the ball), by providing plenty of positive information via press releases (adding water with the cups provided), while stopping the leaks by using ethical resources (with chewing gum or fingers). No unethical means may be used to eradicate the bad press or plug the media leaks (no props may be used to get the ball or fill a hole). You need this done before the expiration of the next 20 minute news cycle. Any questions?

Action: Group attempts to retrieve a ping pong ball from deep inside a leaky pipe by filling the pipe with water.

Intent: Planning, problem solving, decision making, cooperation, communication, trust, and leadership.

Note: Don't do this one indoors, unless in a swimming pool area or able to clean up a lot of spilled water.

Equipment: One 6" diameter 6' long PVC pipe with holes drilled in the sides (about 10 per person) capped and sealed at one end, a ping pong ball, 2 sticks of chewing gum, one cup for two people, and a tap or water supply.

Setup: Position the pipe approximately 30' from a tap or other water source, by sinking it into the ground or hanging it from a tree with the capped end down. Drop the ping pong ball inside it. Gather the group and hand out cups.

Task: To fill the pipe with water, plug leaks with gum or fingers, and remove the ping pong ball as it floats up.

Constraints: You may only use the cups to transport water. You may only plug leaks with chewing gum and your fingers (no clothing or other props may be used). You may not relocate the pipe. You have 20 minutes.

Safety: This activity gets water everywhere, so it is best done outdoors. Watch out for slippery ground.

Facilitation: Unless the pipe is suspended high above the ground, it should not be necessary to fill the entire pipe in order to reach the floating ping pong ball. One can reach in with a long arm and retrieve the ball at about half water height. Therefore, the choice of where to use limited gum and where to use abundant fingers becomes critical to the solution. Debrief for planning, problem solving and decision making. Discuss ethical methods.

Variations: Experiment with the number and size of holes. Limit the water supply to twice the full pipe volume.

63   **Aquaducts/Oil Pipelines**

PROPS: 2   **TIME:** 10-30   **ALIAS:** Bobsleds/Halfpipe, FSII-19
MOVE: 1   **SIZE:** 5-50   **ORIGIN:** Larry Brown

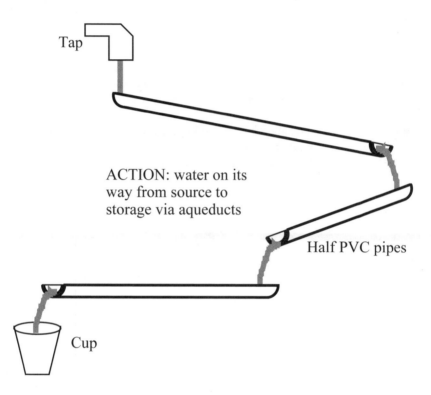

Tap

ACTION: water on its
way from source to
storage via aqueducts

Half PVC pipes

Cup

*Build a pipeline to transport toxic oil (don't touch the water) from the wellhead
(tap) to fill these refinery tanks (cups) before supplies are exhausted (show tap
being turned off) in 30 minutes. The pipeline must be made by connecting these
aqueduct pieces (half pipes) that will be held together by movable stanchions
(each of you). Please notice two things about your route from wellhead to tanks.
First, it is downhill, but not a straight line, so simply interlocking all the pieces
won't work here (pipes can't touch). Second, it is across unstable ground, so
simply resting the pieces on the ground won't work either (you must keep them
above ground). Since the ground is known to move and the tanks may also
shift (spread cups further apart), you will need to devise a means of changing
directions. Quality will be determined by the ratio of amount stored to amount
spilled. Any questions?*

Action: Using short pieces of half pipe (cut in half lengthwise), participants transport water from tap to cup.

Intent: Teamwork, cooperation, communication, trust, leadership, problem solving, and systems thinking.

Note: If doing this indoors, and wishing to avoid the use of water, then substitute a collection of marbles.

Equipment: One half segment of piping per person (1'-2' long), a tap or supply of water (marbles), and 6 cups. Narrower piping makes the task harder. Cut piping lengthwise, so that it is more like a gutter and less like a pipe.

Setup: Position the cups downhill away from the tap, but well within the length of all pipe segments combined. Do not make the obvious route between the tap and cups a straight line: curve it. Turn on the tap with a steady trickle of water. Give everyone their piece of piping. Provide written instructions and/or make this introduction.

Task: To transport maximum water (with minimum spillage) from the tap to cups using a system of aqueducts.

Constraints: You cannot touch the water (marble) and pipes may not touch one another or the ground.

Safety: This activity gets water everywhere, so it is best done outdoors. Watch out for slippery ground.

Facilitation: Initially, people have trouble focusing on two tasks at once (water coming in and water going out) and this makes for an interesting discussion about workloads, attention to detail, caring for others, and systems.

Variations: To make this easier, permit pipes to touch; and to make it harder, prevent people from touching one another. Use diluted syrup instead of water for a slower effect, but get ready to clean up a sticky mess. If getting wet isn't enough, provide suitable consequences for spilling the water. For greater difficulty, make the route go uphill, insert plenty of obstacles to be avoided, and introduce nonverbal or blindfolded constraints. For crisis management, put leaks in one or more cups and attach a movable hose to the tap and change the source location.

64   Shipping by Rail

PROPS: 2   **TIME:** 10-30   **ALIAS:** Chopsticks, UYN-136
MOVE: 1   **SIZE:** 5-50   **ORIGIN:** Clay Fiske

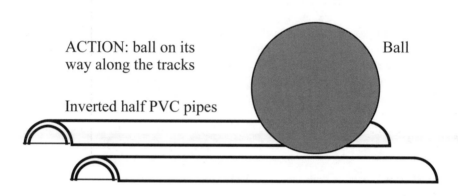

ACTION: ball on its way along the tracks

Ball

Inverted half PVC pipes

In this experience, each of you has half a piece of a railway track (show a pipe segment) and you will need to find a partner in order to make a full length of tracks (demonstrate two parallel segments close together). These trains, carrying your products (balls), can only travel on the tracks from station to station (indicate suitable start and finish points) without interference (no ball touching). If a train gets derailed along its way (ball drops), it must be returned to the starting station to begin again. You know that railway tracks do not move (you may not move your legs when a train is on your tracks), and do not touch one another (people may touch, but your tracks must remain separated). Resources are limited, so tracks may be temporarily deconstructed and reconstructed as needed further down the line (you may only move your legs when a train is not on your tracks). Any questions?

Action: Using parallel short pieces of inverted piping, participants transport a variety of balls from start to finish.

Intent: Teamwork, cooperation, communication, trust, leadership, problem solving, and systems thinking.

Note: If balls are small enough to sit inside a pipe, this problem gets solved like the previous one with marbles. Use larger balls so that double tracks are needed.

Equipment: One half segment of piping per person (1'-2' long) and a variety of different sized balls. Wooden dowelling can be substituted for the piping. Larger balls and thinner pipes or dowels make for a harder task.

Setup: Designate start and finish locations that are much farther apart than the combined length of all the piping pieces. Give everyone their half segment of piping. Provide written instructions and/or make this introduction.

Task: Roll several balls along parallel tracks of piping from start to finish without dropping any balls.

Constraints: You may touch one another, pipes may not. Only the facilitator may touch the balls. You may move to another place only when you do not have a ball on your pipes.

Safety: Avoid feeding balls into the system too quickly as folks panic, tend to run, and flail their sharp pipes.

Facilitation: Discuss the usual teamwork learning and pay particular attention to the systems thinking lessons.

Variations: Permitting pipes to touch makes this task easier and preventing people from touching one another makes it harder. Suitable penalties for train derailments, and blindfolds or nonverbal constraints, may be added. If the route between stations is flat, consider a change to more mountainous terrain (uphill harder than downhill). Have trains coming from different directions and several stations into a single main line with two way traffic and then splitting out again to several other stations. Have natural disasters close the main line so bypasses are made. Add obstacles to the route. Try using one hand per person (two people per halfpipe). Substitute eggs for balls.

65 Trucking to the Showroom

PROPS: 2   **TIME:** 30-60   **ALIAS:** Jelly Roll, SB-134
MOVE: 3   **SIZE:** 5-10   **ORIGIN:** Karl Rohnke & Bob Lentz

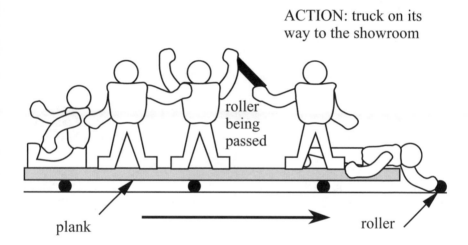

ACTION: truck on its way to the showroom

roller being passed

plank

roller

In this activity, you are trucking your products in groups of five (people) from your factory (start line) to your showroom (finish line). You are using specially designed trucks (planks) with five wheels (rollers) to carry your products. If your truck breaks down (rollers separate from the plank), and you can't get going again within 60 seconds, or if any product falls off a truck, all 5 products must return to the factory to be repaired and trucked again (your group starts over). All products must be at the showroom within 20 minutes. Any questions? GO!

Action: Small groups of five people stand on a plank and move it (by using rollers underneath) over flat terrain.

Intent: Cooperation, competition, problem solving, coordination, planning, and leadership.

Note: This activity requires the use of a flat area. If the ground is slightly sloping, consider using activity #66.

Equipment: A roller per person (1" diameter dowel or heavy duty PVC pipe, 1' long) and a plank (2"x8"x8') per group.

Setup: Mark out an area to be crossed by taping or chalking the start and finish lines about 100' apart. Assemble small groups of five people and distribute their equipment: one roller per person and one plank for each group.

Task: Using a plank with five rollers, to cross a flat open area without falling off the plank or losing any rollers.

Constraints: If your group gets stuck by losing rollers, or if you fall off, all 5 people must return to the start.

Safety: Caution people to keep control of their speed. Discourage jumping to nearby planks that may slip away.

Facilitation: Small groups may sometimes compete (as if this is a race), but the collaborative solution is to share resources and make the crossing more rapidly. If a breakdown happens (rollers are tough to put under a plank with 5 people on top), the only way to get going again is with the help of another small group or by returning to start over. Debrief for competition versus cooperation. Discuss methods used to propel the planks and rollers.

Variations: Ask the groups to maneuver up and down a gentle incline. Place obstacles in their straight paths so that they have to make turns. Provide extra rollers (two per person) and one very long plank for everybody to cross together.

66   **Transitioning to Profit**

PROPS: 3   **TIME:** 30-60   **ALIAS:** Juggernaut, GWA-62
MOVE: 3   **SIZE:** 5-10   **ORIGIN:** British Facilitators via S.P.

plank

ACTION: Advancing
the planks and barrels

barrel

In this activity, you are transitioning through variations in free market conditions (traversing this open area) from a slow economy (start line) to a profitable future (finish line) and this will inevitably be an uphill battle. To make the journey (span the gap), you have information technology (barrels), finances (planks), and human resources (people). Information technology informs you about variations in the free market conditions and so are expected to interact with that situation (only the barrels may touch the ground). Finances enable you to progress, but market conditions can diminish reserves, so keep your money separate from those conditions, in case you have to start over after raising sufficient funds (if planks touch the ground, everyone and everything returns to the start). Human resources dream up and carry out successful strategies, but can become discouraged or depressed by the circumstances, so may need time and your assistance to recover and recreate themselves (people touching the ground will return to the start to begin again, but the group must go back in order to retrieve them). You have 30 minutes to make a profit (get your first person to the finish) before you begin losing market share. Any questions?

Action: Moving barrels across an open area, while balancing people on planks sitting atop the barrels.

Intent: Problem solving, planning, cooperation, communication, trust, support, and risk taking.

Note: This activity requires the use of a slightly sloping area. If the ground is flat, consider using activity #65.

Equipment: Three large plastic barrels (or clean 55 gallon oil drums) and three wooden planks (2"x8"x8').

Setup: Mark out an area to be crossed by taping or chalking the start and finish lines about 50' apart. The area to be crossed should slope slightly uphill toward the finish. Place the equipment at the start and gather the group.

Task: To get people and equipment across an area between start and finish lines without touching the ground.

Constraints: If you touch the ground, only you return to the start. If planks touch the ground, everyone starts over.

Safety: The sloping ground should prevent people from trying to cross by rolling atop barrels on their sides, but consider preventing this practice anyway in order to avoid possible injury. Select a slight slope with soft ground.

Facilitation: Initially, having a person start over (for a person touching ground) has fairly minor consequences compared with everyone starting over (for a plank touch). However, once the group and its equipment is half way across the area, if people return to the start line, the group must waste valuable time returning to retrieve them and this consequence suddenly becomes a major one. When this happens, it is often easier for groups to choose for everyone to start over rather than waste time returning to get one person. Discuss this in relation to staff burnout during tough times at work. Debrief for problem solving, planning, cooperation, communication, trust, support, and risk taking.

Variations: Reduce the ratio of equipment to people for more difficulty and increase the ratio for greater ease.

67   Acquiring New Customers

PROPS: 3   **TIME:** 20-40   **ALIAS:** Trolleys/Skis, SB-118
MOVE: 3   **SIZE:** 2-15   **ORIGIN:** Project Adventure

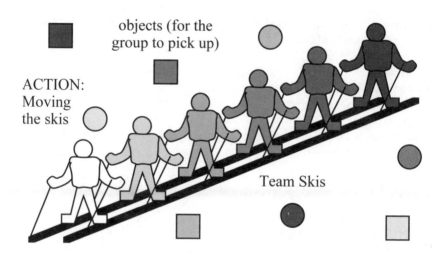

objects (for the group to pick up)

ACTION: Moving the skis

Team Skis

The purpose of this activity is to use your newest ad campaign (skis) to acquire the maximum number of new customers (objects) from this open market (area between the lines) in the shortest amount of time that the ad will run for that market (quickest crossing possible). You are being evaluated by the following formula: number of new customers acquired minus the time taken in minutes. Positive scores (more customers than time) will be rewarded (as determined by facilitators) and negative scores (more time than customers) will have a consequence (also facilitator determined). Everyone must remain committed to the ad campaign when it is running in the market (stay on board the skis when between lines). Anyone who is unable to support the campaign, will be free to exchange their position with someone else who is more supportive (volunteer to change places with another). If the majority can't stand the ad, then all will need to return to this drawing board to create a new ad campaign that can be sustained (if more than half slip off, everyone starts over from the beginning with a new order of people on the skis). Any questions?

Action: Everyone moves together (pulling on ropes attached to the trolley or team skis, while stepping down with their left foot on one and lifting up with their right on the other) through an obstacle course to pick up objects as they go.

Intent: Problem solving, cooperation, coordination, communication, trust, planning, and leadership.

Note: Many versions of these skis exist. The classic version is a long 4"x4" beam with ropes tied into holes drilled through its center. Other versions include aluminum with nylon fasteners holding kevlar wires, or a loop of nylon webbing stitched to one side of old seat belts. Whichever version is used, test that each works safely.

Equipment: A pair of these skis with one space per person, assorted objects (balls, bean bags, etc.), and tape.

Setup: Mark out start and finish lines with tape, spread the objects throughout the area between lines. Place the skis behind the start and assemble the group. Ask them to step into position on the skis and grasp a pair of lines.

Task: To gather the most objects, while travelling through an area (staying on the skis) in the least time possible.

Constraints: If you slip or step off, STOP and have someone change places with that person, before getting back on and continuing. If more than half the group slips or steps off, all of you go back and start over again.

Safety: Spot the people at the very front (they are most likely to slip from being bumped by those behind them).

Facilitation: If everyone doesn't pull together and move in unison, no one will progress forward. Discuss this same revelation at work. Create rewards or consequences for final scores. Debrief for cooperation and planning.

Variations: Use three skis and mix right and left feet on the same ski (so one long ski is common to everyone and the other two short skis move separately like outriggers) with people facing forwards or backwards. Remove all the lines except the first and last ones from each ski, so the group will have to use one another for support.

68   Surviving the Fiscal Year

PROPS: 1   **TIME:** 20-40   **ALIAS:** Stepping Stones, QS-186
MOVE: 2   **SIZE:** 5-15   **ORIGIN:** Unknown, M.G.

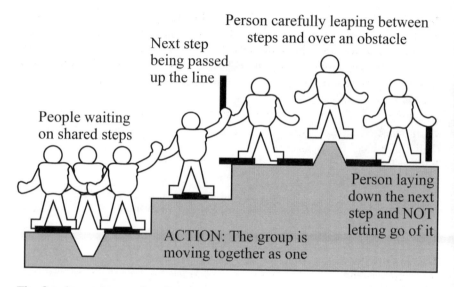

Person carefully leaping between steps and over an obstacle

Next step being passed up the line

People waiting on shared steps

Person laying down the next step and NOT letting go of it

ACTION: The group is moving together as one

The fiscal year is a cycle. Your task is to survive the next fiscal year (make a circuit around this area) by investing your shared finances (placing and standing only on these steps and sharing them as needed). These finances can be invested temporarily, but will remain at a fixed rate, unless you choose to reinvest them elsewhere (steps must remain in place until picked up). If you attempt to shift the rate of return without reinvesting, you will have to delay your survival strategy until the next fiscal year (if you shuffle steps while on them, everyone starts over again from here). If you incorrectly invest your finances (let go of a step), you simply lose that money (you forfeit that step: so maintain constant contact with all steps). Demonstrating leadership brings you a promotion (go to the front of the line). However, anyone making a poor investment will be demoted, and anyone making an illegal investment will be fired (anyone accidentally slipping off steps goes to the back of the line, and anyone stepping off deliberately becomes an observer). If you are unable to work together as a team, you will have to pay a fine (you will sacrifice one step each time an element of teamwork is found to be missing). However, you can collect dividends by showcasing excellent teamwork (you earn back the steps as soon as you demonstrate the missing elements of behavior). I'll be requesting quarterly progress reports on your teamwork. Any questions?

Action: Group circumnavigates a route by only treading on mobile supportive steps that they are carrying.

Intent: Problem solving, cooperation, helping behaviors, trust, support, and communication.

Note: Find a natural area that may be circled by the group (like a pond, a small building or a large room). If unavailable, mark out a route with tape or rope. Select an area (with or without obstacles) that has some elevation changes (such as up and down stairs or moderate inclines). As usual, look for soft ground surrounding the area.

Equipment: One supportive step per person (a plastic plate, carpet square, block of wood, sheet of paper, etc.).

Setup: Gather the group at a suitable location and give a supportive step to each. Hold on to any extras.

Task: To make a single circuit of the area by only treading on stationary support steps and not slipping off steps.

Constraints: Steps are lost if they are left unattended (someone must always be touching each and every step) or if teamwork suffers (as determined by discussion with the facilitator). Steps can be recovered once functional behaviors return (again in discussion with the facilitator). Shuffling steps means start over.

Safety: Spot people balancing in awkward places and encourage them to help one another in these situations.

Facilitation: Intervening to remove a step, or change people's locations, requires an explanation of the shift. If the group wants to argue about it, give them the benefit of doubt (making them aware of actions will usually be enough). Debrief for cooperation and offering or requesting help. Check in regularly for elements of teamwork.

Variations: Split the group in half and send them in opposite directions. Do they share steps when they meet?

69   New Mission Statement

PROPS: 3   **TIME:** 20-40   **ALIAS:** A-frame, SB-126
MOVE: 3   **SIZE:**   5-10   **ORIGIN:** German Facilitators, K.R.

ACTION: Placing the last stick

Asking any group to write a new mission statement usually requires one person to do the hard work of recording all the ideas and reactions from the others. The same applies in this activity: you have chosen a recorder (A-frame operator) who receives supportive input from the rest of the group (who support the A-frame by pulling on their cord ends). The recorder will be expected to write a new corporate mission statement (perform a hidden task) as directed by the remainder of the group. If the recorder is unable to perform the task or role (falls off the A-frame while trying to move), then you will have to go back to square one (start over). Any questions?... If there are no further questions, let me talk to the rest of you over here (away from the recorder).... The mission statement is to make the word TEAM from the sticks in the circle, within the next 20 minutes. You cannot talk about this task to anyone, not even each other. If you talk to anyone, or interfere with the recording process in any way (enter the circle or touch the sticks, recorder or frame), then we will start over. Any more questions?...

Action: Using a stilt-like device (supported by others holding cords), one person performs a task inside a circle.

Intent: Communication, cooperation, coordination, planning, trust, support, leadership, and problem solving.

Note: Construct the A-frame from three 6' long 2"x4" boards. Bolt these together in the shape of a giant A. Test the A-frame with the weight of the heaviest facilitator and then tie all four cords to the top of the A-frame.

Equipment: One A-frame with four 25' cords, thirteen 1' long sticks, and a long rope to mark a wide circle.

Setup: Mark out a 20' diameter circle with the rope and place the A-frame in the circle with the cord ends outside the circle. Randomly spread the 13 sticks around the circle and assemble the group. Ask volunteers to practice moving on the A-frame while the group supports it with the cords. Have the group select their best A-frame user.

Task: For one person operating the A-frame to perform a task as nonverbally directed by the supporting group.

Constraints: Only the A-frame person may enter the circle, touch the sticks, and talk. Others cannot enter the circle, touch sticks, or talk. Infractions, or falling off the A-frame, causes all the sticks to be rescrambled.

Safety: Ask people to hold each cord near its end, so they are always about 15' away from a falling A-frame.

Facilitation: While people assume TEAM will be spelled the same way, many will have a different vision of how the 13 sticks should be formed into letters. This provides for some interesting parallels with writing mission statements or performing tasks, where everyone supposedly knows what it is going to end up like, but they try to get there by different routes. Debrief for communication, cooperation, planning, trust, support, and leadership.

Variations: Other tasks may be used and the task may represent other things. Consider asking people to pull on individual cords. Talking makes this activity easier and asking an A-frame operator not to speak along with everyone else makes it much harder.

70   **Shepherding the Proposal**

PROPS: 2   **TIME:** 30-60   **ALIAS:** Keep It Up, FSIII-49
MOVE: 3   **SIZE:** 5-25   **ORIGIN:** Russian Facilitators, P.W.

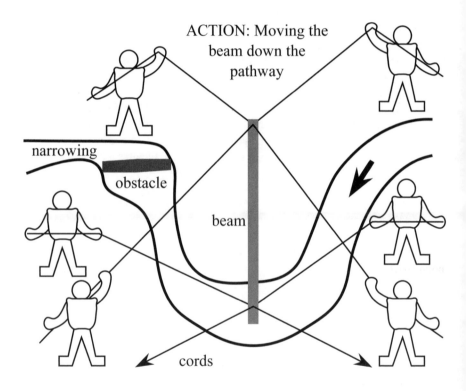

ACTION: Moving the beam down the pathway

Your task is to shepherd this proposal (beam) through the evaluation process (along the designated path) in 30 minutes, coping with any hurdles along the way (overcome obstacles). Use your knowledge and influence (upper and lower cords) to move the proposal along. Do not interfere with the evaluation process or any hurdles (don't touch the path or obstacles), otherwise the proposal will be automatically rejected and you will resubmit it in the next evaluation sequence (start over at the beginning). If the proposal should happen to fail any part of the process, you will need to resubmit a new one (start over if the beam comes off the path). If the proposal falters, simply apply your knowledge and influence (if the beam falls, just stand it up again with the cords). Any questions?

Action: A vertically suspended beam is moved through a obstacle course by people holding supportive cords.

Intent: Cooperation, coordination, problem solving, planning, communication, trust, and support.

Note: The vertical beam gets bounced and dragged along the ground. Do this on a padded surface or outside.

Equipment: One 25' cord for each person (minimum ten cords), a 12' beam (4"x4"), and tape to mark a path.

Setup: Lay out a curved path with tape for the beam to follow. Make the path about 3' wide, but narrow it to 1' or widen it occasionally. To make it challenging, mark the path up or down some hills and over natural obstacles (like running water or fallen logs). Gather the equipment at the starting area. Tie half the cords to the top of the beam and half to the bottom. Assemble the group and ask each person to pick up and hold the end of one cord.

Task: To move the beam through the designated path, and around or over obstacles, within the 30 minute limit.

Constraints: Do not touch the path or obstacles. Keep the beam within path boundaries. If you step in the path or the beam moves out, everyone starts over. If the beam falls, pick it up using the cords. Hold the cord ends.

Safety: Ask people to hold each cord at its very end, so they are always about 25' away from a 12' falling beam.

Facilitation: Discuss typical hurdles at work and how their knowledge and influence is used to cope with these. Debrief for cooperation, coordination, problem solving, planning, communication, trust, and support.

Variations: Allow the group to attach the cords to the beam, but check their knots if this is done. Place bowling pins or traffic cones along the path and if these get knocked down, move the beam back 6' before continuing.

71   One for All & All for One!

PROPS: 1   **TIME:** 20-40   **ALIAS:** All Aboard, SB-106
MOVE: 4   **SIZE:** 10-25   **ORIGIN:** Outward Bound

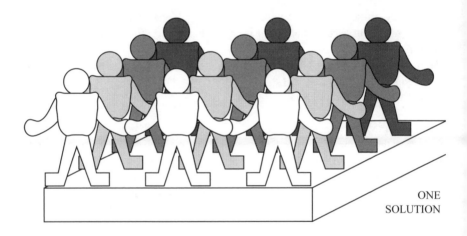

ONE
SOLUTION

Your organization has recently adopted a controversial new management approach and it has been a source of great debate among your employees. The task here is to have everyone demonstrate their commitment to that direction by getting on board with the company's decision (get everyone inside the confined space) without anyone arguing further about it (without talking). Anyone who isn't able to fully let go the old ways, or has one foot in the future and one resting in the past (is touching the ground outside the space), is obviously unable to find a place for themselves with the new mandates and so may get left behind by the group as they move ahead (will be an observer for the next activity we are engaged in). The group may decide who to leave out. Any questions?

Action: Everyone has to fit into a confined space together: standing on a platform or within a circle or square.

Intent: Decision making, problem solving, leadership, cooperation, trust, support, and communication.

Note: The classic version of this uses a wooden platform as the space. Other versions include a taped square on the floor, a rope circle (that shrinks as tightened), and a nylon tarp (that can be folded in half, again and again).

Equipment: A confined space (platform, square, circle, or tarp). Choose and test a suitable size for each group.

Setup: Assemble the group and place the confined space in front of them.

Task: Without talking, to get everyone inside or on top of the confined space and for at least 10 seconds.

Constraints: You cannot touch outside the space. Anyone left out will be an observer in the next activity.

Safety: Spot people if piggybacking is allowed. Do not permit human pyramids or stacking people like cord wood.

Facilitation: Sometimes, a group will be unable to succeed at this task. Perhaps they can get everyone on board for a few seconds, or most people on board for the whole time, but either way then end up with a choice between the group failing, or leaving a few members behind in order for the rest to proceed. This can make for some very interesting discussion and conflict. Discuss how these choices are made at work. Debrief for decision making.

Variations: Continue to reduce the size of the space by shrinking the circle or folding the tarp and challenge the group again (at some point, people may get left behind). Let the group decide the size limits that they can reach.

72   Everyone for Themselves!

PROPS: 2   **TIME:** 20-40   **ALIAS:** Maze, CC-103
MOVE: 2   **SIZE:** 5-15   **ORIGIN:** Project Adventure

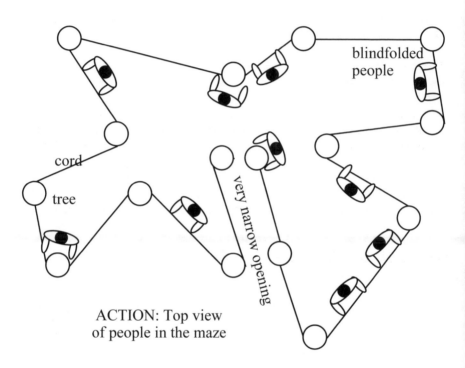

ACTION: Top view
of people in the maze

You are dispersed in a branch of your organization (the maze) that will soon be closing. Anyone who hasn't found a way to get out of this predicament (find the opening) to another branch or position will be fired! Each of you is holding either a severance package (tree) or a job announcement (cord). You can choose to remain here holding the standard severance package or you can choose to search for a new position by following the job announcements. During your search, you may pass several other severance packages and you may choose to remain there or continue searching. At the end of 20 minutes, anyone left at this branch will be terminated, but some will leave with a severance package, while others will leave with nothing. Unfortunately, you cannot see a way for influential friends to help you (so must remain blindfolded). When you have found another opportunity, you will be called by name and told that you have made the move (can remove your blindfold). Any questions?

Action: Blindfolded people find their way out of a maze by feeling their way along cord strung between trees.

Intent: Cooperation versus competition, communication, problem solving, and leadership.

Note: Use an area that has lots of small trees, but is otherwise clear of undergrowth (no sharp shrubs or bushes).

Equipment: One blindfold per person and 300'+ of cord (enough to string back and forth among several trees).

Setup: Create a maze by stringing the single cord between consecutive trees at about 3-4' above the ground level. Find two trees that are close enough together for each group member to fit through the opening. Weave the cords so that this becomes the only exit from the maze. Add several chambers, tight corners, dead ends, and false exits. Blindfold the group away from the maze, lead them there (so they don't see it) and place them separately inside it. Tell them to keep their bumpers up and walk forward until they touch a tree or a piece of cord at waist height.

Task: While blindfolded, get out of the maze by following the cords (or by holding a tree) before the end of time.

Constraints: You must remain blindfolded and in touch with a tree or the cord. You can't duck under that cord.

Safety: Encourage people to keep bumpers up as they move and not to rush quickly head first into one another.

Facilitation: Is this performed with everyone for themselves or do they work together to save others? Debrief for cooperation versus competition. If someone has found the way out and wants to reenter the maze, consider what the rules for reentry should be (perhaps reblindfold people and place them randomly back inside or allow them to reenter the same opening that they used to get out of the maze). What does rescuing represent at work?

Variations: Close the opening entirely and the only way people can get out is by asking for help (the first step to any personal change process).

73   **Quality is a Journey**

PROPS: 1 **TIME:** 30-60 **ALIAS:** Gridlock, ZG-58
MOVE: 1 **SIZE:** 5-20 **ORIGIN:** Rocky Kimball

SETUP: A master grid map of the best way through

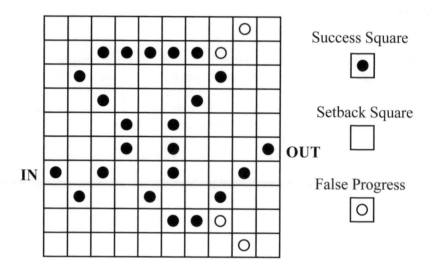

Nonverbally, you will take turns to find a quality path from mediocrity (this side) to excellence (the far side) through a pattern of successes and setbacks (the grid route). Quality is defined as the fewest acceptable setbacks in the shortest elapsed time. Both will be measured by a quality inspector (facilitator or group member with the map and noise makers). During your turn, if you are on the quality path (stepping on success squares), you will not receive feedback from the quality inspector (no noise) and may continue searching for excellence. If you step off the quality path (onto setback squares), you will receive this feedback (make suitable first noise here) and must return to mediocrity to await your next turn. Making such mistakes the first time is a valuable learning opportunity and will be rewarded without penalty. However, the need to revisit prior learning (step on the same setback again later) will result in additional feedback (make suitable second noise) and a costly relearning penalty of one minute added to your final completion time. The route may be found by stepping to adjoining squares only (demonstrate options). Dead ends may give an illusion of false progress: pick your path wisely. Any questions?

Action: People take turns trying to discover the hidden route through a grid of about 100 squares.

Intent: Teamwork, trust, cooperation, communication, leadership, decision making, and planning.

Note: For a more complex problem, the grid can be composed of triangles or other shapes instead of squares.

Equipment: Tape to create a grid on the carpet or a prefabricated grid on a large tarp. Noise makers are optional.

Setup: Unroll the tarp with the prepared grid or use a roll of tape to create one on the carpet. Square dimensions should be about 1' by 1' and 100 squares (10 by 10) is ample for a group of ten people. Create a master map of the route through the grid and use that map to track people's progress or note where they step off the route.

Task: To move the group across a grid by stepping on nearby success squares and by avoiding repeat steps on to setback squares.

Constraints: Conduct this nonverbally. Take turns: one on the grid at a time. Only move to adjacent squares. Success means continue. Setback means return to start. Repeated setbacks bring a one minute penalty added to overall time.

Safety: Watch for people who get dizzy and often lose their balance taking careful steps among tiny squares.

Facilitation: Keep track of the group's progress and where they step off (so repeats can be noted) on the master map. Debrief for communication, cooperation, decision making and other typical teamwork lessons.

Variations: To make the task easier: use verbal communication; avoid using dead ends; allow many people to follow a leader; and permit the group to make maps or use coins to mark the route. Break large groups into small ones, have them enter and exit the grid at different points, but reverse their route back out after each setback.

74   Gather a Group Together

PROPS: 3   **TIME:** 60-120   **ALIAS:** Jail Break, NEW
MOVE: 4   **SIZE:** 10-20   **ORIGIN:** Australian Facilitators, S.P.

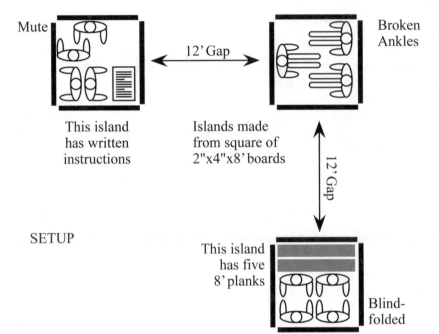

Mute

12' Gap

Broken
Ankles

This island
has written
instructions

Islands made
from square of
2"x4"x8' boards

12' Gap

SETUP

This island
has five
8' planks

Blind-
folded

WRITTEN INSTRUCTIONS: You may only whisper to one another so the others cannot hear you and you must nonverbally communicate this written information to the other two subgroups. This activity is about gathering your entire group together in one place. Everyone in a subgroup (on different islands) has strengths and weaknesses. The task is to bring everyone together with you by bridging the gaps between your strengths and weaknesses (building plank bridges and crossing over to your island). You have difficulty communicating (mute), but can see the bigger picture (have this information). Some have trouble moving from their views (bound ankles), but are excellent as intermediaries (translate between mute and blindfolded). Others have trouble seeing a bigger picture (blindfolded), but can be counted on to get the work done (only ones allowed to touch planks and so may have to carry everyone else). If anyone does another's work (touches a plank while not blindfolded), or if members or materials should get side tracked (a person or plank touch ground outside an island), these members or materials will experience a major setback (returned by the facilitator to the farthest island away). You have one hour to gather your group. Any questions?

Action: Three subgroups on islands attempt to build connecting bridges and overcome difficult restrictions.

Intent: Communication (within and among groups), strengths and weaknesses.

Note: This is an advanced version of activity #35. Islands are made by laying the four 2"x4" boards in a square.

Equipment: Twelve 8' long 2"x4" boards, five 8' long 2"x8" planks, and a blindfold for each person.

Setup: Place the islands about 12' apart (so that one 8' plank can't stretch between them) in a curved line or L-shape. Put the five planks on an end island. Break the large group up into 3 subgroups: blind, mute, and bound ankles (allow folks to choose: the blindfolded may be carrying other people). Place the blind group on the island with the planks, the bound ankles group in the middle, and the mute group on the other island. Announce to everyone that more information will be coming soon and give the written instructions opposite to the mute group only.

Task: To get everyone together onto the mute island by building bridges between all islands before time runs out.

Constraints: You may not leave your islands except by building bridges. The mute subgroup may not speak to other subgroups (who may speak to anyone). Only the blindfolded may handle planks, anyone who gets bumped by a plank gets penalized. If a plank or person touches ground outside an island, they get penalized. The penalty is a reversal move at the facilitator's discretion (planks can go back to the mute island, and people can be sent to the blindfolded island).

Safety: Watch for blindfolded handling planks. Spot people as they carry others.

Facilitation: Allow the group to discover that the planks are too short to bridge the gaps and so they must come up with a solution. This involves counterbalanced bridges where one person walks out on a partially extended plank, while the others counterbalance it by standing on one end. If a plank touches someone who is not blindfolded, take it away and announce the rules again. Discuss some of the more common miscommunications that arise: statement inaccuracies and details; not sharing all the information; accidental penalties; and not allowing everyone to play a part in solving the problem.

Variations: Since time can be spent waiting for both bridges to be built, have unexpected work tasks (occupying activities #4-15) for some subgroups to do.

75   Data Download

PROPS: 1   **TIME:** 20-40   **ALIAS:** Electric Fence, QS-208
MOVE: 4   **SIZE:** 5-30   **ORIGIN:** K. Rohnke, Brahm Schatia

ACTION: Center person
is climbing on others
to get over the rope

rope

post

You are a sequence of data that may choose to adopt any arrangement (you can change your order) and means of connection (you don't have to hold hands as long as you maintain physical contact by other means). Download this sequence on your corporation's network (cross over this rope) from their company's server (this side) to the customer's laptop computer (that side), without corrupting the network or the data sequence along the way (touching the rope means you start over). You may not use any other unauthorized networks to transmit data (people may not pass under the rope), but you may use other networks to support the data transmission (temporarily reach or extend your body under the rope). Breaking the connection results in termination of the transfer and loss of important data, so the data will need to be resequenced and transmitted again (everyone returns here to start over). Any questions?

Action: Without breaking contact, a line of connected people cross over a horizontal rope without touching it.

Intent: Trust, support, cooperation, communication, leadership, planning, problem solving, and helping others.

Note: The original Electric Fence activity had a remarkable number of injuries due to people vaulting or being thrown over the upper wire. The newer Nuclear version has made some adjustments to reduce this possibility.

Equipment: A length of rope or bungee cord. An area with two trees or posts, surrounded by soft ground.

Setup: Suspend the rope or bungee cord horizontally between the trees or posts, so its lowest point is an average 3' above the ground (waist height). Gather the group on one side of the rope and ask them to join hands in a line.

Task: To cross over a rope (3' off the ground) without touching the rope or breaking contact with one another.

Constraints: Everyone must pass over the rope, and may temporarily reach out under the rope to help others. Constant contact with one another must be maintained. Start over if you break the connection or touch the rope.

Safety: Encourage people to use others for support while they are crossing over the rope, and not to lose contact with one another during passage. People can reach under the rope to help the first and last person in the line.

Facilitation: Debrief for trust and support. Discuss communication, cooperation, and helping behaviors.

Variations: For a more difficult task, do not allow reaching under the rope. Lower the rope to make the task easier, but never raise it above average waist height. Instead, consider placing a second horizontal rope about 3' above the first one, so people must pass between both ropes. Do NOT discard or forget the constant contact rule as this keeps people safer by being supportive.

76   Conflict Resolution

PROPS: 3 **TIME:** 30-90 **ALIAS:** Croc Pit, BB-41
MOVE: 4 **SIZE:** 5-15 **ORIGIN:** Australian Facilitators, S.P.

ACTION: One very light person crawls out on
the plank in order to position equipment....

...while the rest of the group sits on a
crossbeam in order to counterbalance

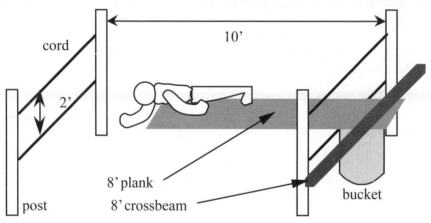

cord

10'

2'

8' plank
8' crossbeam
post
bucket

These are your resources: support (buckets), risk taking (planks), and trust (beam). Your task is to get you and your resources through the discord (through the cords) and over the disharmony ahead (over the area in between posts) without being caught by minor disputes (touching cords or posts) or drawn into major conflicts (touching the ground in between). If you or your resource gets caught by a dispute, that person or resource will return for conflict resolution training (anyone or anything touching cords or posts returns to the start). If you or your resource gets drawn into a conflict, then the whole team and all of its resources will return for retraining (if anyone or anything touches the ground in between, everyone and everything will start over). Any questions?

Action: People crawl on counterbalanced planks across a confined area, and between and through two pairs of horizontal cords.

Intent: Problem solving, cooperation, communication, trust, support, risk taking, planning, and leadership.

Note: For this activity, soft ground (grass) is an added advantage in case anyone falls or gets dropped. The equipment must be strong enough to support the weight of several people. If in doubt, use aluminum materials.

Equipment: Two 30' lengths of bungee cord or string, four posts (or 6' wood stakes), two very strong buckets (sturdy milk crates or heavy wooden boxes), two 2"x8" planks (6' and 8' long), and a 4"x4" beam (8' long).

Setup: Arrange the posts (or insert the stakes into the ground) to layout a 10' by 10' square. Tie a bungee cord or string horizontally between two posts so that one cord is 3" below the height of a bucket (crate or box) and the other is about 2' higher than that. Duplicate this obstruction at the other end. Gather the group.

Task: To get people and equipment across an area, without touching the ground, and through obstructions, without touching these.

Constraints: You must go between the two cords. Any people or equipment that touches the cords or posts, is returned to the start. If a person or equipment touch the ground, then everyone and everything will start over.

Safety: Keep all body parts from being placed underneath the boards in case of falling or being dropped.

Facilitation: Neither plank will stretch the 10' gap and a bucket cannot be placed in between as a center support. One solution involves counterbalancing planks with the combined weight from most of the group. One lighter person crawls out onto 7' of extended plank, resting on a first bucket, while seven heavier people put their combined weight on a crossbeam atop the remaining 1' of plank. This allows the light person to position the second bucket on the far side, outside the gap, and then move the second plank to bridge that gap. Debrief problem solving, communication, and planning. Discuss the roles played by real support, risk taking, and trust in the actual resolution of conflicts.

Variations: To make this task easier, consider dropping the lower cord to ground level or raising the upper cord. To make the task more difficult, introduce more obstructions (made from cord and posts) to the area in between.

77   **Distribution Network**

PROPS: 3   **TIME:** 30-90   **ALIAS:** Spider's Web, CC-106
MOVE: 4   **SIZE:** 5-20   **ORIGIN:** John Jarboe

ACTION: Person being passed through the web by four other supporters (two on each side). Notice that the head is being carefully held by two people to prevent neck hyperextension.

You will be sending shipments (people) through a distribution network (web) from the warehouse (your side) to my retail outlets (my side) within the next hour. Each of my outlets is located in a different state and so each shipment (person) will need to take a different routing (through his or her own opening in the web). If two shipments share the same route, I will return both of them to your warehouse for you to sort out my order (both people who passed through the same opening will start over). If any shipper or shipment should collide with the network during transport (anyone touches a strand while passing a person), then that shipment will be suspect and should be returned for repair and reshipment. However, your own quality control must identify these suspect shipments and take them back voluntarily, because if you deliver damaged shipments to any of my outlets and we both know they have been damaged (a person is passed through after touching a strand), then I will return every shipment ever sent me (everyone starts over) and we will renegotiate our contract of 60 minutes. Any questions?

Action: People get passed by the group through the openings of a giant web without touching any of its strands.

Intent: Problem solving, planning, cooperation, communication, trust, support, quality control, and leadership.

Note: This activity uses the classic Spider's Web that is created by weaving bungee cord and/or string between two posts or trees to create a giant web with plenty of openings (at least one per person and perhaps more) that are also large enough to pass people through.

Equipment: Two posts or trees (surrounded by soft ground), and a large amount of bungee cord and/or string.

Setup: Weave the web with at least one opening (various shapes and sizes) large enough for each person in the group. Gather people on one side of the web, as you stand on the other, so that the web is in between you and the group.

Task: To get everyone through the web in 60 minutes without touching the strands or using any opening twice.

Constraints: You cannot go over, under or around the web: you must go through it. Each person should go through a different opening. Using the same opening twice returns two people to the start. Contacting the web during passage through the web by anyone (even the supporters) returns only the person being passed to the start. If that person is not taken back voluntarily after a touch is noticed, then everyone starts over.

Safety: Make sure the head and neck of people being lifted are well supported. Encourage people to lift with their legs and not their backs. Remember challenge by choice and have alternate quality control or observer roles for some.

Facilitation: Play the role of customer with great gusto. Success in this activity requires advance preparation for who goes through which opening and in what order. Debrief for planning and a wide selection of teamwork lessons.

Variations: Allow a few free touches or some openings to be used more than once. Have the group pass objects through extra openings. Ask the group to create their own web design beforehand. Try a three dimensional web.

78   **Labor Negotiations**

PROPS: 3 **TIME:** 30-90 **ALIAS:** Meuse/Acid River, CC-87
MOVE: 3   **SIZE:**   10-20 **ORIGIN:** Paul Radcliffe

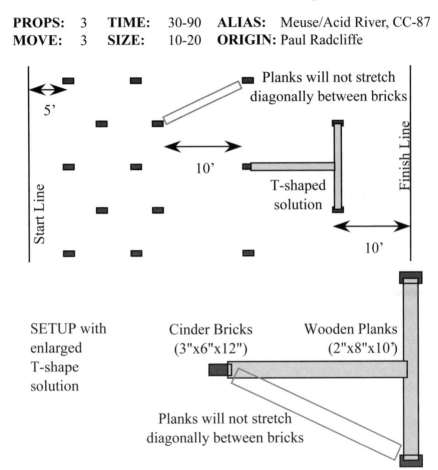

As I understand this situation, management wants to reach a fair settlement (finish line) by participating in labor negotiations (crossing open area) from your present position (start line). What were your requests for the settlement again?... Okay. So to do this, you will be using your negotiation tools (planks) to reach several minor agreements along the way (bricks) without any major misrepresentations that might delay everyone's progress (if anyone steps off a plank onto the ground, then both subgroups must start over). Negotiations must be associated with the intent to agree (planks must rest on bricks) and not misrepresent (if a plank rests for more than a few seconds on the ground, both subgroups start over). Any questions? REPEAT THIS FOR THE UNION SUBGROUP.

Action: People cross an open area by walking on planks that rest on bricks.

Intent: Conflict resolution, adversarial collaboration, problem solving, trust, and communication.

Note: While cinder bricks are often used in this activity, wooded blocks or paper sheets can add to its portability.

Equipment: Four planks (2"x8"x10'), 15 bricks (4"x6"x12"), and tape or rope for start and finish lines.

Setup: Layout the bricks as shown in the diagram (note that the gaps between earlier bricks are easily bridged by a plank, but gaps between later bricks cannot be crossed with one plank alone: two planks must make a T-shape. Position start and finish lines 5' and 10' away from the nearest bricksrespectively . Divide the group into two subgroups of 10 people (union and management in this example). Assemble at the start, give each subgroup two planks, and brief them separately.

Task: For both subgroups to get across the open area by only walking on planks and resting planks only on bricks.

Constraints: Everyone starts over for resting a plank or stepping on the ground.

Safety: Caution people to handle the planks with care and to avoid hitting others or dropping planks on them.

Facilitation: Two adversarial subgroups, briefed separately, are likely to compete. They will race across the first few bricks with ease. When they encounter the place where the gap is too wide for one plank, one subgroup will figure out the T-shaped solution and the other may choose to copy it. Once all ten members of a subgroup are standing on both of their planks, they cannot progress further unless they choose to work together with the other subgroup. This is the time to allow them the freedom to really negotiate. Debrief for the metaphor of union and management working together to reach a fair settlement. During the crossing, any mistakes will impact both subgroups and this can add to their disagreement. Discuss how the actions of one may influence the other during labor negotiations and what strategies could be used to collaborate.

Variations: For more difficulty, make subgroups larger or use one plank per subgroup. Using an odd number of subgroups, and not an even number (3 rather than 2), may result in the abandonment on one subgroup and the discussion of some interesting issues. For ease of movement, provide a rope to adjust planks.

79   Executing a Strategic Plan

PROPS: 3   **TIME:** 30-60   **ALIAS:** Zig Zag, SB-124
MOVE: 2   **SIZE:** 5-10   **ORIGIN:** Karl Rohnke, Mary Todd

SIDE VIEW of a MODIFIED 6' (4"x4") beam with two feet of 2"x4"x6" blocks

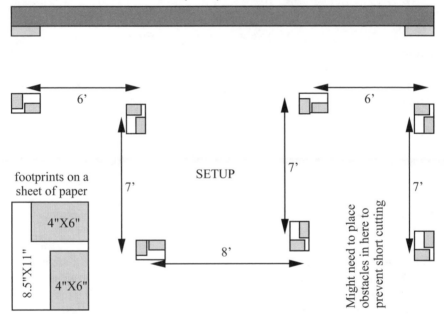

Your group is charged with the task of executing your piece of the strategic plan. This piece has 8 goals (segments) for your group to accomplish using these three strategies (beams). Each strategy must be correctly positioned in order to achieve each goal in sequence and effectively lead the way toward the next (beams must be placed entirely on a paper sheet, the long axis of which points to the next sheet). If a person or strategy loses the perspective while attempting to reach a goal, then the whole plan will need readjusting (if people or beams touch ground, or are not resting on a paper sheet during a crossing, then everyone starts over again). Any questions?

Action: People travel a zig-zag route across an open area by laying down different sized beams in precise places.

Intent: Problem solving, planning, trust, dealing with unexpected surprises, communication, and cooperation.

Note: Each of the three beams listed below are modified by nailing two small blocks (2"x4"x6") to either end of the same side of a beam, so as to create short footings to keep the non-flexible beam off the ground as in the diagram.

Equipment: Three 4"x4" beams (6', 7' and 8' long) MODIFIED as shown opposite, 7 sheets of heavyweight paper, and tape.

Setup: The small blocks have a footprint of 4"x6" and two footprints will fit on a single sheet of paper. Build a sequence of eight segments by taping paper islands to the floor, so that each segment is just wide enough to span with a beam between islands (like 6'-7'-8'-7'-6'-7' as diagrammed) and segments are oriented at right angles (with the long axis of a sheet pointing to the next island). Once the sequence is ready, assemble the group.

Task: To place 3 beams on 7 paper sheets in order and to walk on the beams across the gaps between sheets.

Constraints: If you or a beam touches the ground, and is not resting on the paper, everyone starts over.

Safety: Caution people to handle the beams with care and to avoid hitting others or dropping beams on them.

Facilitation: Groups typically stand on two beams and move one. A surprise comes when a beam doesn't fit or span the length and they must readjust to stand on one beam and move two. Discuss dealing with the unexpected.

Variations: Number the paper sheets and have the sequence cross over itself once or twice in a tight area. To prevent shortcutting between sheets, place obstacles in the way or draw the footprints on the paper with arrows pointing to the next number. Ask that these be followed exactly. Have a route that branches and rejoins later on. Make longer or shorter sequences as needed.

80   **Insured Objectives**

PROPS: 4 **TIME:** 30-90 **ALIAS:** Mohawk Walk, CC-101
MOVE: 3 **SIZE:** 5-15 **ORIGIN:** Karl Rohnke, Mohawks

ACTION: Group moving across a segment of cable

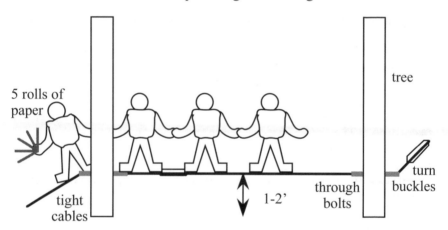

In front of you is your next corporate venture with several objectives (a series of cable segments). Some earlier ones are easier (shorter) and can be completed individually, while other later ones are harder (longer) and require the group to work jointly on the objective. Objectives are interdependent, so if you fail to reach any one objective (fall off at any point), you will need to start from the first one and repeat all objectives (begin again from the start). However, since a new start up is costly, we have purchased five insurance policies (5 rolls). These policies underwrite all startup costs and enable you to return to just before the slip-up, so use these thoughtfully (surrendering one policy mean only repeating the last segment, not all the previous segments). Any questions?

Action: Group supports one another as they maintain contact to walk across a series of tight ropes or cables.

Intent: Decision making, cooperation, coordination, risk taking, trust, support, and helping behaviors.

Note: Many versions of the Mohawk Walk exist. The classic version is several cables strung between tree bases, less than 2' above soft ground. The cables are anchored to bolts drilled through the tree trunk and are tightened by a turn buckle. More portable versions include wooden planks screwed into base platforms, tight ropes stretched around posts, or aluminum rails with side buttresses. Whichever version is chosen, test that each works safely.

Equipment: A Mohawk Walk facility (as described above) and five rolls of paper (held with elastic bands).

Setup: Check the safety of the facility, assemble the group at one end of the walk, and give them 5 paper rolls.

Task: To get from start to finish by walking atop tight cables, while supporting one another to avoid falling off.

Constraints: Falling off means the group starts over from the very beginning. Using one of the five insurance policies means returning to repeat only that last segment and continuing on with the remaining segments.

Safety: Spot people in the middle of the longer segments. Encourage those who lose their balance to simply step off and not to try and fight the momentum until they are lying flat on the ground. Make sure the surrounding ground is soft.

Facilitation: People who try to cross the cables alone soon realize that they reach a point where the group must work together to support one another. The more difficult decisions involve when and where to make an insurance claim. Obviously, using up the rolls on earlier falls doesn't gain much advantage, but saving them until the end means they may never get used. Striking this balance, and the decision making process to reach it, makes for interesting discussion afterwards. Debrief for cooperation, risk taking, trust, support, and helping behaviors.

Variations: Instead of limiting the number of falls, assign time penalties and state a time deadline for finishing. Ask the group to carry objects with them that afford greater protection or increased consequences for falling off.

81 **Partner Trust & Support**

PROPS: 4 **TIME:** 30-60 **ALIAS:** Wild Woosey/V, CC-110
MOVE: 3 **SIZE:** 2-10 **ORIGIN:** Peter Bryant

ACTION: Two partners moving along the 'V'
(spotters not shown for clarity). Spot people!

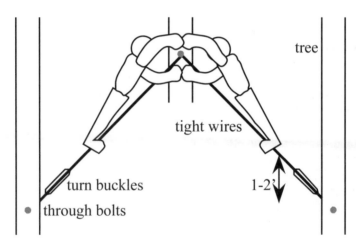

*Your group has the goal of raising $1,000,000. Each of you has one opportunity
to contribute $100,000 by working in partnerships for this activity. Please select
a partner who approximates your size and weight.... Okay, now that all ten of
you are partnered up, your task is to stand on these two cables as a pair. While
facing one another, grasp hands to support one another, but without interlocking
fingers. Now lean forward and move down the diverging cables toward the trees
at the far end. Your group will receive $100,000 for each person who reaches a
tree. If both partners make it together, your group will receive a $50,000 bonus (a
total of $250,000 per pair). However, if you fall off the cable, you will receive a
percentage of the award based on how far you travelled along the cable ($50,000
for half way). You can do the math and decide the best paired order to follow.
You may change partners, but only if the partners have not yet had a turn and the
group agrees. Any questions?*

Action: Two people support one another, while walking atop diverging cables and slowly moving further apart.

Intent: Risk taking, trust, support, consensus decision making, planning, and cooperation versus competition.

Note: Many versions of the Wild Woosey exist. The classic version is two cables strung between tree bases, less than 2' above soft ground, in a diverging V-shape. The cables are anchored to bolts drilled through the tree trunk and tightened by turn buckles. More portable versions include aluminum rails with side buttresses and retaining wires or wooden planks screwed into base platforms. Whichever version is chosen, test that each works safely. Spotting for this activity can be very different from the norm and should not be attempted without proper training.

Equipment: A Wild Woosey facility (as described above) and a stack of play money ($5,000 minimum bills).

Setup: Check the safety of the facility and then assemble the group at the narrow converging apex of the V.

Task: To lean against your partner and to walk (one pair at a time) along the diverging cables toward the end.

Constraints: Partners are usually picked through friendships or allegiances, and sometimes people feel left out. Swapping partners can only be made by group consensus and among partners who have not yet had their turn.

Safety: Caution pairs to keep their heads on opposite sides to avoid striking faces together should they both fall. Remove jewelry and sharp objects. Get help in spotting this activity: it takes a unique combination of positioning and commitment. Recall challenge by choice and give folks another role to play if they do not wish to participate.

Facilitation: Whether the partners change or not is often a more interesting dynamic than their efforts to succeed on the cable. Although all are working toward a common goal, some people can't resist competing with their coworkers. Discuss the roles and responsibilities of work partners. Debrief for risk taking, support, and trust.

Variations: One popular version is to perform this activity 30' above the ground with safe belaying procedures. Consider changing the monetary award amounts.

82

Trading Places

PROPS: 4   **TIME:** 30-60   **ALIAS:** Whale Watch, QS-192
MOVE: 2   **SIZE:** 10-20   **ORIGIN:** Pam McPhee and others

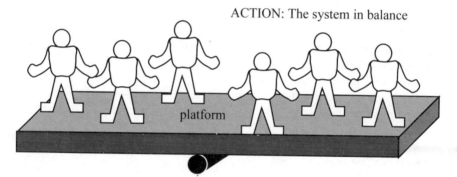

ACTION: The system in balance

platform

balance log

Tomorrow your organization will be hosting its first Job Empathy Day, where employees get a chance to temporarily switch positions with their co-workers in an effort to appreciate what one another's job entails. Since you are concerned enough to make sure the work still gets done and that the company doesn't plunge into turmoil and chaos, I will be pilot testing this concept with your group today. I would like you to exchange positions with your partner without destabilizing your organization (swap places on the platform without unbalancing it). You can afford 5 simulated destabilizations in this pilot, but after that we will cease testing (when the platform touches ground a sixth time, the activity is over). I would also like you to practice your partner's job by role playing each other (as you move, say or do one thing that your partner would commonly say or do). Any questions?

Action: The group balance on a giant platformed teeter totter and then switch positions without unbalancing.

Intent: Problem solving, planning, cooperation, communication, trust, support, and leadership.

Note: This activity uses a facility called the Whale Watch, that is simply a large platform pivoting back and forth on the central fulcrum of a large log. Originally designed to accommodate wheelchairs, this platform has replaced the standard teeter totter where one person falling can topple everyone. Avoid using this like playground apparatus.

Equipment: One Whale Watch facility (as described above)

Setup: Ask the group to step onto the Whale Watch. Ask people to find their own places where the platform can be balanced so that the ends on either side are not touching the ground. Ask them to pick a partner on either side.

Task: To change places with your selected partner in a controlled manner that does not unbalance the platform.

Constraints: The platform cannot be held to prevent its tipping. You have 5 free ground touches. After these expire and the platform contacts the ground again, the activity is finished. Role play your partner's behaviors.

Safety: Encourage people to move slowly and not to place any part of their bodies underneath the platform.

Facilitation: Discuss the actions of individuals or groups that can lead to destabilization. When people role play one another, take care to foster an atmosphere that prevents negative defaming or discounting, and be prepared to talk about this with the group. Debrief for problem solving, planning, cooperation, communication, and trust.

Variations: Ask people to take turns stepping on in pairs and moving to their respective balance points. Ask them to get off in the reverse of this. Ask everyone to stand over the center balance point and move to within 2' of the ends and then move back to the middle again. Ask them to stand around the perimeter of the platform and then perform a circular walk around the outside staying with 2' of the edge and returning to their original places. Ask them to lie down and then stand up again without tipping the platform. Ask them to try one blindfolded.

83   **Replacing a Defective Part**

PROPS: 4   **TIME:** 30-60   **ALIAS:** Tired Pole, CC-115
MOVE: 4   **SIZE:** 5-20   **ORIGIN:** Outward Bound

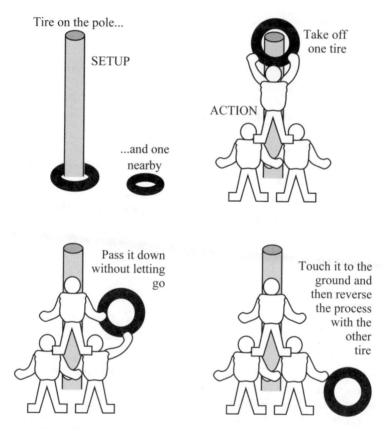

Once in a while, even your best products get returned for replacement of defective parts under warranty. In this activity, you will replace a defective part (remove one tire and replace the other) from one of your popular products (pole). Health and Safety Regulations prevent workers from coming into direct contact with the product once this particular part is being removed, so please avoid doing so (no one may touch the pole). Environmental Protection Guidelines demand that both the old defective part and the new replacement part be handled to avoid damaging the workplace, so please treat these parts with extreme care (maintain constant contact with both tires). Inspectors will stop your work for an infraction and require you to start over from the beginning. Any questions?

Action: By climbing on one another, the group removes a tire from a vertical pole and then replaces another tire.

Intent: Risk taking, trust, support, communication, cooperation, problem solving, and planning.

Note: Inform folks that the activity requires people to step and climb on one another: challenge by choice applies.

Equipment: A 12' vertical pole (buried 3' into the ground, so the top is 9' above ground level) and two old tires.

Setup: With the group watching, toss or place one tire over the pole and lay the other on the ground nearby.

Task: To remove a tire, touch it to the ground, and replace another tire over the pole, without touching the pole.

Constraints: Start over if you touch the pole, or if you fail to maintain constant contact with both tires.

Safety: Teach people the basics of safely climbing on one another with compassion. Anyone leaving the ground should be spotted by those not otherwise involved. Stop any unsafe acts. Supervise and promote spotting.

Facilitation: Play the role of inspectors. Discuss CARES (Concern, Awareness, Respect, Empowerment, and Safeguards) for coworkers and the workplace. Debrief for risk taking, trust, support, cooperation, and planning.

Variations: Higher poles can be used, but this is probably inappropriate for all but the most physically fit folks.

84   **Constant Patient Care**

PROPS:	4	**TIME:**	30-60	**ALIAS:**	The Spool, CC-91
MOVE:	4	**SIZE:**	5-20	**ORIGIN:**	Outward Bound

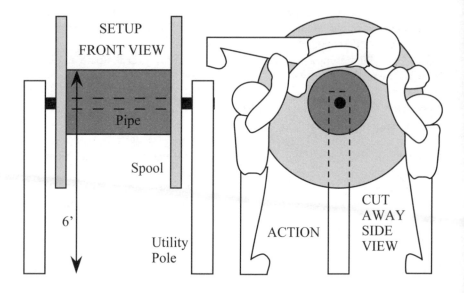

In your hospital, patients are cared for constantly and so is the case in this activity. Patients (people) will be processed from admissions (this side), through treatment (over the spool), to discharge (the other side). At all times, the patients' needs must be cared for (by maintaining constant contact with the person passing over) and all their concerns must be addressed (with encouraging language and behaviors). However, you are implementing a new peer support program where patients will do this for one another. Any patient who fails to receive this level of care (letting go of someone before they are over or not lifting the last person) will need to be readmitted (person starts over). So, the first patient may not have help for discharge and the last may not have help with admissions. A discharged patient cannot reverse treatment (cannot go back over the spool) to admissions. Any questions?

Action: The group passes people over a rotating spool from one side to the other with constant contact.

Intent: Anticipation, support, problem solving, planning, cooperation, trust, communication, and risk taking.

Note: This activity uses a giant cable spool mounted on a horizontal steel pipe axle (supported by two vertical utility poles) so that the top of the spool's center is about 6' off the ground. The spool rotates around the pipe.

Equipment: A Spool facility as described above. Do not use this activity with a group that is not prepared physically or as a team.

Setup: Check that the spool spins freely and that the ground is soft. Check overall safety and gather the group. Explain what the activity will entail and offer alternate observation roles for voluntary non-participants (challenge by choice).

Task: To get everyone over the spool, while making sure that each person is cared for according to the constraints.

Constraints: Constant contact and supportive language and behavior must be given to the person going over the spool. If not, that person starts again. You cannot return to the start, once you have already successfully crossed the spool.

Safety: Identify places that people should avoid getting pinched by the spool. Remove jewelry or sharp objects.

Facilitation: Getting the first one over is easy (as long as someone keeps constant contact with him or her), but getting the last one over can be difficult. If the group forgets, and the second to last person goes over and lets go of the last one, that person is stranded and the activity is finished. Debrief for support, anticipation and planning.

Variations: Do away with the contact rule and allow people to return back over for a much easier solution.

85   **Wholesale to Retail**

PROPS: 4 **TIME:** 30-60 **ALIAS:** The Beam, IG-15
MOVE: 4 **SIZE:** 5-20 **ORIGIN:** Military, Outward Bound

CAUTION: No more than two on top, with everyone spotted!

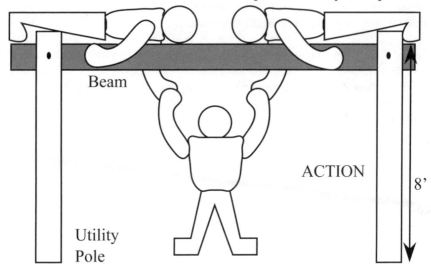

You are responsible for freighting goods (people) from the wholesaler (this side) to the retailer (that side) over a high mountain pass (over the beam). No routes exist around the mountains or through a tunnel (can't go around or under) and no off-road shortcuts are allowed (can't touch the side poles). If your trucks (people) need a rest at the top of the pass, they will only find two spaces there. Extra trucks will need to continue downhill or a resting one will need to move on and leave room for a new one to rest there. Trucks can only assist others on their side of the pass (you can only lift people on your side). For safety, all trucks should stay in radio contact with any truck on the mountain (people must spot anyone who is off the ground). The only way back to the other side, is to return over the pass (go back over the beam again if you want to). Goods must be delivered in 30 minutes. Any questions?

Action: The group passes people over an eight foot high horizontal beam from one side to the other.

Intent: Anticipation, support, problem solving, planning, cooperation, trust, communication, and risk taking.

Note: This activity uses the Beam facility, which is simply a horizontal utility pole through bolted between two vertical utility poles, so that the top of the beam is about 8' off the ground. The beam should be sanded smooth.

Equipment: A Beam facility as described above. Do not use this activity with a group that is not prepared physically or as a team.

Setup: Remove splinters and knobs from the surface of the beam. Check overall safety and gather the group. Explain what the activity will entail and offer alternate observation roles for voluntary non-participants (challenge by choice). Caution participants to have snug fitting and well fastened clothing, so nothing gets inappropriately pulled off.

Task: To get everyone over the beam safely without violating any of the constraints discussed below.

Constraints: You cannot go under the beam, only over. You can't use the side poles for assistance. Two on top of the beam (with a third going over) is the limit. Everyone else must be spotting these three at all times, with special attention given to anyone hanging beneath the beam. You can only touch, lift, or hold someone on your side (can't reach under and help the other side). You can't return to the start, unless you go back over the beam.

Safety: Spotting is critically important. If people fail to spot, safely stop the activity and start again. If the group repeatedly fails to spot, stop again and do a different activity. Remove jewelry and any sharp objects in pockets.

Facilitation: Anticipating how to get the last person over (without anyone to lift him or her) is the crux for this problem. Debrief for this anticipation, problem solving, and planning. Discuss trust, support, and risk taking.

Variations: This activity becomes more a right of passage if people are allowed to return under the beam to help out as needed.

86   Insurmountable Obstacles

PROPS: 4   **TIME:** 30-60   **ALIAS:** The Wall, CC-113
MOVE: 4   **SIZE:** 5-20   **ORIGIN:** Military, Outward Bound

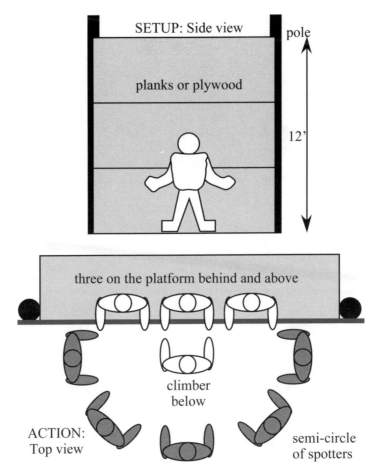

SETUP: Side view

pole

planks or plywood

12'

three on the platform behind and above

climber
below

ACTION:
Top view

semi-circle
of spotters

*I'm interested in knowing what this group sees as its most insurmountable obstacle
for the future.... Okay, this wall represents that seemingly insurmountable obstacle.
Your challenge is to work together and find a way for everyone to overcome this
obstacle. Get your group over the wall according to these restrictions. Only 3
people on the platform at a time. Don't hang with your head lower than your
knees. No using props or parts of the wall for help. Constantly spot anyone on
the wall until they are standing on the platform. Any questions?*

Action: The group passes people over a high wall on to a platform behind.

Intent: Anticipation, support, problem solving, planning, cooperation, trust, communication, and risk taking.

Note: Do not use this activity with a group that is not prepared physically or as a team. This can be a very physical activity and is best used with fit groups. A less strenuous alternative is activity #87. Remove jewelry and sharp objects.

Equipment: A Wall facility is 12' high with a platform and ladder on the back side. It is built by bolting 8' planks or plywood sheets between two utility poles.

Setup: Check overall safety of the Wall and gather the group. Explain what the activity will entail and offer alternate observation roles for voluntary non-participants (challenge by choice). Caution participants to have snug fitting and well fastened clothing, so nothing gets inappropriately pulled off.

Task: To get everyone over the wall (the crux involves getting the last and first people over with limited help).

Constraints: When the capacity of three on the platform is exceeded, one of the four people must descend the back ladder (with spotting). After descending, that person must come and help spot at the front, but may not lift anyone. No hanging with the head lower than the knees (upside down) at any time. Using extra props (clothing, belts, or branches) or the support poles, cracks, knot holes, or the sides of the wall for help is not allowed.

Safety: Check the ladder is well footed and secured to the platform. Spot people as they descend the ladder as this is where injuries are most likely. Also, spotting should be done by forming a semi-circle around the person going over, with extra spotters on the sides. Insist on high quality spotting and attention to safety by all during this activity. If in doubt, stop and go do something else.

Facilitation: Two hanging positions are acceptable and necessary for the typical completion of this activity: feet first and hands first. One person (with another holding on) hangs from the top of the wall and dangles the feet. Another leans over (but never with head below the knees and again with another person holding on) and extends hands downward toward the climber. This last person climbs the body of the first until a hand can be grabbed from the second.

Variations: Taller walls up to 15' high have been used, but a wall under 12' is probably best for corporate groups.

87   Ascending to a New Order

PROPS: 4   **TIME:** 30-60   **ALIAS:** Mineshaft, BM-145
MOVE: 4   **SIZE:** 5-20   **ORIGIN:** Simon Priest

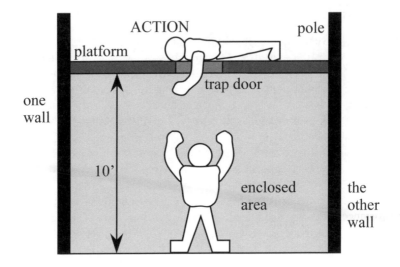

Your organization is evolving from old directions to new visions. For any company to evolve, its groups will need to contribute their growth to that evolution. In this activity, your group will be growing from the present (under the platform) to the future (above and on the platform). For the group to grow, its members will also need to contribute their personal changes to that growth (so plan your sequence in advance). Each of you will be thinking about changing something personal. When it is your turn to grow with the group and evolve with the company, I'd like each of you to verbally share one of your personal changes. Also ask your group how they can help you to accomplish it. Any questions?... HOW? Oh, how you get up on top is for you to figure out. You can't exit the door through which you entered (the past) and you can't climb up the outside to reach the platform. GO!

Action: The group passes people up through a small (initially hidden) trap door onto a large platform.

Intent: Anticipation, support, problem solving, planning, trust, cooperation, communication, and risk taking.

Note: This activity uses a Mineshaft facility. The Mineshaft is a horizontal platform (about 10' above ground level) built between two vertical Walls (see #86), so it is like a small enclosed room with a deck on top (and a door to get in). A small (approximately 2' by 2') trap door is cut in the platform and hidden by the construction joists.

Equipment: A Mineshaft facility as described above. Do not use this activity with anyone who will not fit through the trap door.

Setup: Check the trap door can be easily removed and is concealed. Check overall safety and gather the group. Explain what the activity will entail and offer alternate roles for voluntary non-participants (challenge by choice).

Task: To get everyone onto the platform, through the small trap door (the crux is getting the last person through).

Constraints: Share your personal goal for change with the group and ask them for assistance achieving it.

Safety: Encourage people to look straight ahead when being pulled up through the trap door, because looking upwards can cause them to bang the back of their heads against the roof. Remove jewelry and sharp objects.

Facilitation: Initially people will not understand how to get on top, but once they discover the trap door, the rest follows easily. Remind them to make their personal change statement before getting lifted. Getting the last person up is much easier than with activities #85 or #86. The platform allows one to lie down and reach through the opening to grab the jumping last person. People on top can squat (rather than bend) and pull with their legs (rather than their backs) to raise the last one. Discuss what the trap door represents at work.

Variations: Leave the trap door open. Place a heavy weight on top of it, so the group has to work harder.

88   Courier Delivery

PROPS: 3   **TIME:** 30-60   **ALIAS:** Nitro Crossing, CC-104
MOVE: 3   **SIZE:** 5-15   **ORIGIN:** Outward Bound

ACTION: Second from last person swinging
on the rope and receiving the glass of water

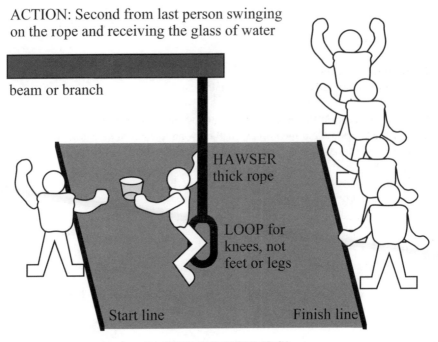

beam or branch

HAWSER
thick rope

LOOP for
knees, not
feet or legs

Start line   Finish line

OUT-OF-BOUNDS!

In this activity, you will be delivering packages (people) from your business offices (this side) to your customer's homes (that side), using this sophisticated courier service (hanging hawser). One extremely fragile package (glass) must be delivered without loss of contents (spilling the water). If these contents spill, then all packages will be returned to your offices and everything will need to be resent by courier (everyone starts over). If any package fails to reach its destination (person touches this middle area), then it will need to be returned for redelivery (just that person starts over). You may customize the courier (tie knots) as you like. Any questions?

Action: Several people swing across a defined area on a suspended rope and also transport one glass of water.

Intent: Problem solving, communication, cooperation, trust, support, and leadership.

Note: This activity requires that a rope, suspended from a high anchor (like a beam or a tree branch), support the weight of swinging people (physical forces will be much greater than simply hanging on the rope). If unsure of how to select anchor points or determine rope strengths and physical forces, please find an expert who can help.

Equipment: Glass of water (or beans if indoors), two 20' ropes (to mark two lines), and a hawser (thick rope).

Setup: Tie a loop in the hawser. Locate the anchor point and attach the hawser so that the loop stretches within 1' of the ground. Complete a few test swings to determine the overall safety of the system and to position a start and a finish line (made with two ropes). Designate the area in between as out-of-bounds and gather the group.

Task: To swing everyone, plus a glass of water, across an area without touching down or spilling the water.

Constraints: Any person touching the out-of-bounds area (including accidental stepping over either line) must start over. Spilling the water means everyone starts over. You may tie multiple knots in the hawser as you like.

Safety: Do not allow people put their foot through the loops, suggest they use their knees. Give people some practice holding onto the hawser before they are expected to swing on it. Avoid people stepping on one another's backs. Remember challenge by choice and allow non-swingers to observe. Remove sharp objects and jewelry.

Facilitation: Sometimes, the first challenge lies in retrieving the dangling hawser. Debrief for problem solving and creativity associated with this and the other challenges of getting specific people and the glass of water across.

Variations: Narrow the space between start and finish lines to ease the task. Designate tight landing spaces (islands or platforms) to add difficulty. Consider blindfolds, muting or broken limbs as possible handicaps.

89 Corporate Ladder Climbing

PROPS: 2 **TIME:** 10-20 **ALIAS:** High Ladder Climb, NEW
MOVE: 4 **SIZE:** 5-10 **ORIGIN:** Asian Facilitators via S.P.

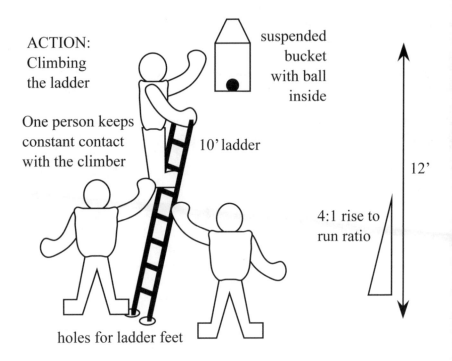

ACTION: Climbing the ladder

suspended bucket with ball inside

One person keeps constant contact with the climber

10' ladder

12'

4:1 rise to run ratio

holes for ladder feet

In this activity, the group is supporting one person who is seeking to obtain a promotion (ball) within the organization (bucket) while climbing the corporate ladder. How can we physically support someone looking for a promotion?... Okay, these ways of supporting will be represented by everyone holding the corporate ladder and at least one person maintaining constant contact with the promotion seeker when climbing the ladder. And what are some things we might say to encourage someone to go for that promotion?... Okay, when the person is on the ladder, you may only say positive encouraging words like the ones we just talked about. Any questions?

Action: Group supports a ladder while one person climbs to remove a ball from a suspended bucket.

Intent: Risk taking, trust, support, cooperation, communication, problem solving, and decision making.

Note: This activity has been done with much higher ladders and belaying, but keep it short and simple.

Equipment: One 10' ladder (no longer), one bucket containing a ball, and some string to tie the bucket in place.

Setup: Suspend the bucket (with the ball inside) from a tree branch (so that it is about 12' above soft and flat ground). Be sure the bucket is placed well away from anything that the ladder might be rested on for advantage. Lay the ladder on the ground and assemble the group. Explain that one person will climb the ladder, while the others hold it still. Ask them to pick a climber and decide whether they want to hold the ladder or just observe.

Task: To climb the ladder and remove the ball from the bucket, while the rest of the group supports the ladder.

Constraints: At least one person must maintain constant contact with the climber. Use positive language only.

Safety: Dig two shallow holes as anchor pits for the ladder feet. Request that the ladder slope be less than a 1:4 rise to run ratio (a line dropped from the top of the 10' ladder will be about 30" away from its base).

Facilitation: Help the group brainstorm some non-verbal and verbal actions that support others. Discuss the notion of teamwork versus individual promotions. Debrief for support, trust, encouragement, and risk taking.

Variations: Mark out an area that the base of the ladder and people must remain within. Have them use negative discouraging language first and then compare the climber's two language experiences in the debrief afterwards.

90 Making Defect-free Widgets

PROPS: 2 **TIME:** 30-60 **ALIAS:** Pick and Choose, SB-77
MOVE: 2 **SIZE:** 10-100 **ORIGIN:** Karl Rohnke & Lee Peters

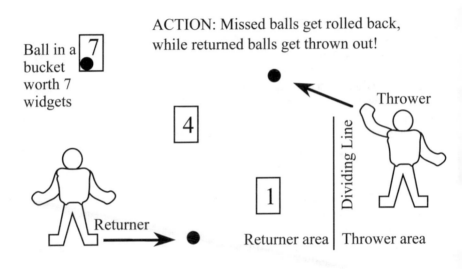

In this activity, you will be making widgets during 5 production shifts (2 minutes long) and discussing how to improve your process in 4 planning sessions (5 minutes long) in between those shifts. You are interested in reaching optimum production levels for this system by the end of 5 production and 4 planning times (30 minutes). Each group has one shift supervisor (an observer) and nine workers, with twice as many widget producers as inspectors (6 throwers and 3 returners). At the start of each shift, producers will be making widgets by injecting these replicators (buckets) with precursors (balls). Each replicator then creates the number of widgets shown on its label. All defects (balls on the ground) will be returned (rolled back) by the widget inspectors to the producers who will reinject these precursors. All workers must remain at their designated work stations during each shift (no returners in the thrower area and visa versa) and are not properly cross trained to do the other's job (throwers can only touch balls behind the dividing line and returners cannot redirect balls into buckets). At the end of each shift, I will quickly provide you will production data to help you with your next planning session. The planning sessions will be managed by your supervisor (observer) and the next shift will begin on time. Any questions?

Action: Groups strategize and work together to throw balls into buckets across varying distances and elevations.

Intent: Planning, problem solving, systems thinking, collaboration, leadership.

Note: This is better done in a large room (without breakable windows) or outside with a backstopping wall.

Equipment: Ten buckets, tape or rope (to mark boundaries), a felt-tipped marker, flip chart, and 10 soft balls per person (tennis balls work very well).

Setup: Mark out a dividing line with tape or rope so that 10% of the floor space is a thrower area and 90% is a returner area. Place the 10 buckets around the returner area at varying distances from the throwing area and in various elevations above the throwing area. Assign point values to each bucket based on how difficult it might be to throw a ball into (from 1 = easiest to 10 = hardest) and write these values on the buckets with the marker. Assemble everyone in the thrower area and ask them to break into groups of ten people. Then ask each group of ten to select six ball throwers, three ball returners, and one observer who will not be touching any balls.

Task: To design and execute a system that allows optimal production of widgets within the limits of the system.

Constraints: Planning and production times, workers roles and locations, buckets and boundaries are all fixed.

Safety: Make sure the balls are soft, because throwers often hit returners.

Facilitation: After each shift, record the number of balls in each bucket, multiply these by the respective bucket values, sum these subtotals, and report the total for that production cycle on a large chart while the group is still engaged in their planning session. Have a few helpers count balls and restock the throwing area between shifts. After the first shift, the groups will likely want to make changes to the system. Determine whether each change is permissible (8 throwers and 1 returners) or not (moving any buckets closer). Make answers congruent with the essence of the widget production analogy given above. Debrief for differences in supervisors' leadership styles and for collaboration among groups. Discuss communication, planning, and systems thinking.

Variations: To make this more competitive, give different colored balls to each group of ten and keep score by group.

91 Group that Blows Together

PROPS: 2 **TIME:** 30-60 **ALIAS:** Team Blowgun, ZG-166
MOVE: 1 **SIZE:** 5-10 **ORIGIN:** Sam Sikes and others

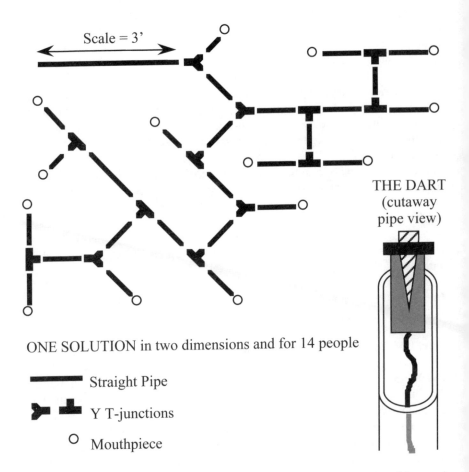

Scale = 3'

THE DART
(cutaway
pipe view)

ONE SOLUTION in two dimensions and for 14 people

———— Straight Pipe

➤ ⊥ Y T-junctions

○ Mouthpiece

*This is a two phase problem. First, imagine and create a team vision (blowgun)
using materials selected only from the limitations (pipe segments) you have been
given. Second, use your team vision to deliver a most inspirational message (dart)
to your target audience of employees (hoop or paper). To be successful, everyone
in your group must agree on the vision and its use, and you must all work together
(blow) at the same time in order to communicate on target. You will contribute
from your own unique perspectives (mouthpieces). Any questions?*

Action: The group works together to build a team blowgun and then blows in unison for accuracy and distance.

Intent: Teamwork, cooperation, communication, planning, coordination, problem solving, and creativity.

Note: Be certain everyone has their own clean mouthpiece for this. The actual design (2 or 3 dimensional) is not as important as the way in which the group blows together to achieve coordinated accuracy and distance.

Equipment: A dart (made of wood dowel, with a felt disk screwed into the top and an attached string tail); a few targets (hula hoops or paper); and an assortment of PVC piping segments of various lengths (at least one 3' long and the others shorter); T or Y-junctions (adding a few angles); and couplers (for use as individual mouthpieces).

Setup: Give all materials to the group and either provide written instructions or give the following introduction.

Task: To construct a blowgun with one mouthpiece per person and then blow together to hit a target with a dart.

Constraints: Use only the materials provided, no need to use every piece, but everyone must be able to blow and have their own individual mouthpieces. The blowgun cannot be moved closer than 30' from the target.

Safety: Clean and dry all materials (especially mouthpieces) really well in a solution of diluted bleach before and after each use. Encourage contagious folks with colds or the flu to observe and report back during the debrief.

Facilitation: Strong members will blow back weaker ones and this makes interesting metaphoric discussion. Also discuss the usual teamwork lessons that commonly arise and share learning from any observers present.

Variations: Can be conducted non-verbally and with some group members blindfolded. Let the group assign new goals for distance or accuracy and attempt to break records. Vary the type of darts; avoid sharp points.

92   **Build a Better Mousetrap**

PROPS: 2 **TIME:** 30-60 **ALIAS:** Mousetrap, EM-115
MOVE: 1 **SIZE:** 5-10 **ORIGIN:** Sam Sikes

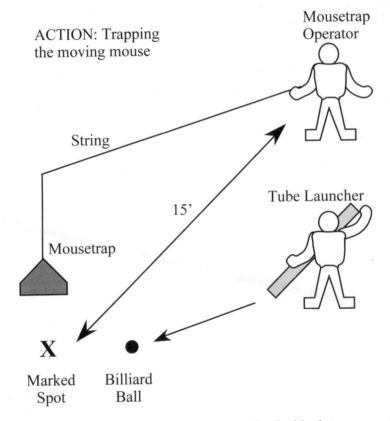

ACTION: Trapping the moving mouse

Mousetrap Operator

String

15'

Tube Launcher

Mousetrap

X
Marked Spot

Billiard Ball

Your research and design firm has been contracted to build a better mousetrap. Your department has 30 minutes to build a live trap version from these materials. After that, a mouse (billiard ball) will pass by here about every minute for the next 10 minutes, thus providing you with ten attempts to catch the mouse by testing your new version. The mouse will be moving at various speeds and in different directions, but can always be expected to pass over this point (marked X) during its travels. The trap must be operated remotely (from a distance of at least 15' away), must catch the mouse alive (cannot crush or spike the ball), and must prevent it from escaping through any holes (openings must be smaller than the 2" diameter billiard ball). Any questions?

Action: Group builds a structure that can be operated remotely to trap a moving billiard ball.

Intent: Planning, problem solving, success versus failure, communication, and cooperation.

Note: Expect all versions to vary from the one diagrammed below. Equipment could be used in activity #91.

Equipment: Ten sheets of paper, masking tape, thread, several rubber bands, one billiard ball, an assortment of PVC piping (segments of various lengths: at least six 2' pieces; eight 1' pieces; twenty 3" pieces; six elbows; six T junctions; and two couplers), and a 4' long tube (4" diameter, that all the equipment can be stored inside).

Setup: Place a marked X on the floor and create a launcher from the tube. Be sure the ball will roll through the tube so that it reliably crosses the marked X from any direction and at most speeds. Assemble the group.

Task: To build a trap that will stop a ball moving across the floor according to the designated specifications.

Constraints: Ball speed and direction will change, but it will always cross the X. The trap must be triggered from over 15' away, make a live catch, and prevent the possible escape of the ball after being caught.

Safety: Do not roll the heavy ball toward people or anything else that might be breakable.

Facilitation: Vary the tube's incline to adjust the ball's speed and its angle to modify the ball's direction. If the mark is missed, don't count that attempt against the group and simply send the ball again. Debrief for planning.

Variations: Send multiple balls and ask the group to catch one or all of them. Reduce the amount of materials.

93   **Target Audience**

PROPS: 2   **TIME:** 30-60   **ALIAS:** Catapult, NEW
MOVE: 1   **SIZE:** 5-10   **ORIGIN:** Sam Sikes

EQUIPMENT

SETUP

work area

hula hoop

tarp

You have two target audiences: a specific population (hula hoop) who are seeking your product (so are located close by) and the general population (tarp) who are not yet aware of the product (located far away). Your task is to create an advertising mechanism (catapult) from the resources available (materials set) that will deliver an ad (payload) from your offices (work area) to both of the target audiences so that you can make a sale (payload must touch the hoop or tarp in some way). You have several possible types of ads that can be delivered (a variety of payloads). You have a limited advertising budget (can only launch each type of payload 5 times), but test ads cost full value (1 launch). A correctly chosen and delivered ad could reach both target audiences. Any questions?

Action: Group builds a catapult that hurls various payloads to hit two targets in different distances or directions.

Intent: Problem solving, leadership, teamwork, communication, cooperation, trust, planning, and execution.

Note: The materials listed can be used to build the transportation vehicle in #36.

Equipment: A selection of payloads (golf, tennis, nerf, soccer, foot, basket, and baseballs), two targets (hula hoop and tarp) and one materials set composed of: 2 wheels with axles; two 6' long 2"x2" boards (with 0.25" holes drilled at various places along their lengths); 2"x4" boards (two 8', four 4', and eight 2' long, also with 0.25" holes); two 2'x4' pieces of 0.5" thick plywood (with 0.25" holes drilled around its edges); a ball of twine; a knife; 3' of bungee cord; paper and pen (optional); and a large open space like a playing field or gymnasium.

Setup: Put everything in one corner of the field (gym), the tarp in the opposite corner and the hoop in the middle.

Task: To contact two targets by launching a variety of payloads from a catapult (maximum 5 launches per payload).

Constraints: Payload must touch the target (hit it directly, bounce onto it, or roll into it). Catapult must stay in the work area, but may be repositioned as desired. Facilitators may move targets and return launched payloads.

Safety: When testing or using the catapult, even without a payload, clear people well back from the launch area.

Facilitation: There are two problems here: building a catapult and using it to hit both targets. Debrief how well ideas were shared for both tasks. Discuss issues which arise from the usual leadership and teamwork learning. Some groups will create slingshots or crossbows (thinking these are catapults): decide in advance if this will be acceptable. Also, determine in advance whether the group will be able use their own resources (like clothing) to enhance their designs.

Variations: Footballs are usually launched as the last resort because of their seemingly random bounce pattern. Add other oddly shaped balls to the payload selection. Add further consumables such as masking and duct tape. To make the task easier, move targets closer to one another and toward the work area. To make the task harder, move targets farther away and place them out of alignment. Consider changing the designation of completed hits.

94   **Quality Benchmarking**

PROPS: 2   **TIME:**   30-60   **ALIAS:**   Tower Building, NEW
MOVE: 1   **SIZE:**   5-10   **ORIGIN:** Canadian Facilitators, S.P.

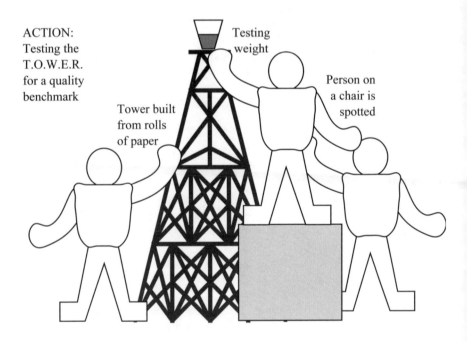

ACTION:
Testing the
T.O.W.E.R.
for a quality
benchmark

Testing
weight

Person on
a chair is
spotted

Tower built
from rolls
of paper

*Your task is to use these materials (no other props) to build the forerunner of a
new product line: the Tall Ornament With Extreme Rigidity (the T.O.W.E.R.). The
quality benchmark is for this product to support the testing weight at a height of 6'
above ground for 60 seconds. You have 30 minutes before any structural testing
begins. Planning may be done verbally, but building must take place nonverbally.
Any questions?*

Action: Group builds a single tower for height and strength that will surpass the quality benchmark.

Intent: Planning, problem solving, communication, cooperation, and quality control.

Note: If doing this inside, substitute beans for water in the cup. If outside, find a place sheltered from the wind.

Equipment: A collection of building materials (limited quantities of newsprint, cardboard, paper, elastic bands, pens, glue, tape, paper clips, string, stapler and staples) and one testing weight (plastic cup with water or beans).

Setup: Assemble the group and provide the collection of building materials and the testing weight.

Task: To build a tower that will support the cup of water for 60 seconds at a height of over 6'.

Constraints: No talking during construction. Use only the materials provided.

Safety: Have the group spot and/or support anyone who stands on a chair to gain a height advantage.

Facilitation: Debrief for planning, problem solving, communication, cooperation, and quality control.

Variations: Decrease the height and increase the duration or visa versa. Provide a wider variety of materials.

95   **Seamless Programming**

PROPS: 2   **TIME:** 30-60   **ALIAS:** Bridge It, SB-127
MOVE: 1   **SIZE:** 10-20   **ORIGIN:** Australian Facilitators, S.P.

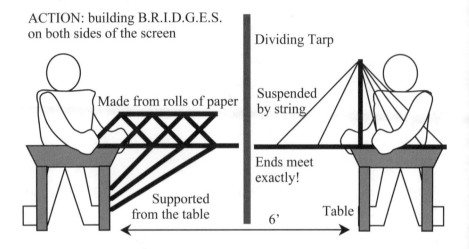

ACTION: building B.R.I.D.G.E.S.
on both sides of the screen

Dividing Tarp

Made from rolls of paper

Suspended by string

Supported from the table

Ends meet exactly!

6'

Table

Your task is to use the resources to create a new training program called Bold Reaches Into Distant Gaps by Emergency Spanning (B.R.I.D.G.E.S.). Each consultancy (half group) will create their half of this program (bridge half) in their respective areas of expertise. Unfortunately, both consultancies are widely separated and so can only communicate by telephone (radio). The two halves of the program must be different to address different training needs, however, one half must start up exactly where the other leaves off (bridge halves must look different and must span a 6' gap by meeting at exactly the same point on the dividing tarp). In about 60 minutes, we will unite the two consultancies to demonstrate their training programs (by dropping the tarp) and we will be paying particular attention to the breadth of learning (6' span), a lack of need for external support staff (not resting on the floor only connected to the tables) and seamless programming (exact connections). Any questions?

Action: Two groups separately build two halves of a bridge and later see how closely the two join up.

Intent: Planning, problem solving, communication, cooperation, trust, support, and quality control.

Note: The best facility for this is one room with a separating curtain divider drawn across to make two rooms.

Equipment: Two sets of building materials (limited quantities of newsprint, cardboard, paper, elastic bands, pens, glue, tape, paper clips, string, stapler and staples), an opaque 8'x20' tarp, two tables, and two radios.

Setup: Hang the opaque tarp vertically to divide the room in half. Split the group in half and place each half in opposite sides of the room. Provide each half group with one set of building materials, one table and one radio.

Task: To build two halves of a bridge that meet in the middle at exactly the same location and span a 6' gap.

Constraints: Tables must be at least 6' apart, materials may not touch floor (only tables), talk using radios only.

Safety: If the radios have long antennas, caution people to be careful where they point these.

Facilitation: Stop the action and drop the tarp after 60 minutes, unless extra time has been negotiated. Compare bridge halves and examine the point of connection. Debrief for communication, planning, and problem solving.

Variations: Have the half groups speak two different languages and provide translations sheets (up means down, right means left, etc.). If radios, walkie-talkies or cell phones are unavailable, let the whole group or elected representatives meet to discuss their work in a distant location where they cannot see either half of the bridge.

96   **Workforce Integration**

PROPS: 4   **TIME:** 60-120   **ALIAS:** Troubled Waters, NEW
MOVE: 4   **SIZE:**   10-40   **ORIGIN:** Simon Priest & Mike Gass

ACTION: crossing the bridge over troubled waters,
while wearing a PFD: Personal Flotation Device

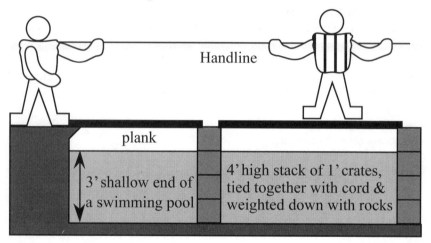

*Your half groups exemplify small parts of two much larger and different cultures
at work in the same newly merged corporation. Your task is to establish common
bonds between your cultures (build a bridge across the pool) and then to integrate
your joint workforce (by sending all of both groups across the bridge). Establish
common bonds using identical resources at your disposal (use the equipment
available). Integration should be conducted one worker at a time, but you may
have multiple workers in transition (take turns sending a person over the bridge
to the other side, but you can have more people on the bridge at any time). Full
integration is required within 60 minutes (everyone must have changed over to the
other side at least once by then). Any questions?*

Action: Groups on either side of a swimming pool build a bridge across the pool and then switch sides across it.

Intent: Problem solving, planning, communication, cooperation, trust, risk taking, and leadership.

Note: This activity requires a swimming pool (use the 3' deep shallow end with a flat bottom and cross width ways). Employ a lifeguard and provide enough PFD's for people on the bridge and those getting ready to cross.

Equipment: Various lengths of wood planks (enough to exceed the pool width), numerous stackable milk crates or a suitable substitute (enough to stand on the pool bottom and stack to a height of 4' to make central supports), several clean rocks (or heavy weights to hold down the floatable crates), 100' of string to tie it all together, and PFD's (4-6 worn by the people while crossing or preparing to).

Setup: Split the group and equipment in half and place each half on opposite pool sides at the shallow end. Refer to challenge by choice and offer people an opportunity to observe rather than risk getting wet in this activity.

Task: To build a bridge of planks across the pool with support from the pool sides and central milk crate stacks.

Constraints: Crossing is recommended one at a time, but you can decide how many to allow on the bridge. No short cuts around the outside of the pool or across corners to the end (the bridge must be built straight across).

Safety: Do this well away from the end of the pool so falling people can't hit the end, and consider padding the pool sides with ethafoam. Ask everyone who stands over the water or on the bridge to wear a PFD.

Facilitation: Sometimes groups will use all the string for construction. Others will save enough string to make a balance line, so crossing the shaky structure is much more steadily performed. Discuss multiple resource uses and feelings of alliance to one half group over the other. Debrief for inter-group communication and sharing.

Variations: A suspended tire in place of a central support and one less plank than needed makes for a very challenging task.

97   **Passenger Transportation**

PROPS: 3   **TIME:** 60-120   **ALIAS:** Raft Building, IG-17
MOVE: 3   **SIZE:**   10-20   **ORIGIN:** Outward Bound

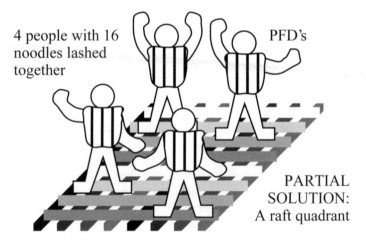

4 people with 16 noodles lashed together

PFD's

PARTIAL SOLUTION: A raft quadrant

Your industry manufactures mass passenger transportation vehicles of all shapes and sizes: rapid transit; airplanes; and ferries. Your task here is to construct a new vehicle with a capacity of 20 (or the exact group size). The vehicle must be made from strong lightweight materials (noodles and string) and be extremely maneuverable. In 60 minutes, you will take your constructed vehicle through a test track (water course chosen by facilitators) and demonstrate its performance. If it passes muster, I'm confident you'll sell many in the future. Any questions?

Action: Group constructs a raft from ethafoam noodles and paddles it around a short test track with their hands.

Intent: Planning, problem solving, communication, cooperation, trust, risk taking, support, and leadership.

Note: The original version lashed planks and barrels together and had to be accomplished before the tide came in over the local sand bar. This can still be done with planks and barrels, but the results are apt to roll over, so try the noodles. This activity requires a body of water (a pond or swimming pool). Provide PFD's and a lifeguard.

Equipment: One PFD and four ethafoam noodles for each person, and a ball of string for lashing it all together.

Setup: Bring the group to the edge of the water and distribute the equipment to them. Remind people to wear their PFD's. Refer to challenge by choice and offer people an opportunity to observe rather than risk getting wet.

Task: To construct the raft and maneuver it through a testing route as chosen by the facilitators.

Constraints: Noodles and string are the only construction materials (other props and PFD's must not be used to build anything).

Safety: When in or on the water, people must be wearing their PFD's. Tell folks they should expect to get wet.

Facilitation: Typical raft designs involve making a quadrant by lashing 8 or 10 noodles at right angles across another 8 or 10 noodles. Four quadrants combine to make a raft of about 8'x8' that holds about 16-20 people. Whether it stays together during maneuvers is another matter. On the test track, ask them to carry the raft over obstacles, launch it into water, and paddle it forwards, backwards, sideways, in circles, and through tight spaces without crashing. Once the raft has been built, some groups realize that they didn't consider propulsion and have nothing left to make paddles with and so must use their hands. Debrief for planning, trust, and problem solving.

Variations: Provide paddles, very limited quantities of string, and fewer noodles to make this more challenging. If moving water (not necessarily white water) is available, or a strong wind, an advanced test might be conducted.

98   **Hostile Takeover**

PROPS: 3   **TIME:** 60-120   **ALIAS:** Plane Crash, NEW
MOVE: 2   **SIZE:** 20-100   **ORIGIN:** T. Dixon, Mindee Naismith

blindfolded leader
carrying resources

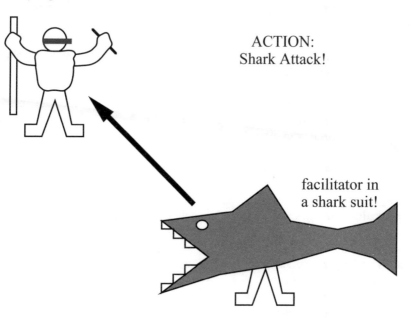

ACTION:
Shark Attack!

facilitator in
a shark suit!

WRITTEN INSTRUCTIONS: A hostile takeover is in progress and you have four tasks to accomplish. First, gather resources. Only mobile leaders can do this, while you remain in your offices (stay put) and provide direction. Second, defend against attrition. Use these incentives (insulated noodles, electric wires and batteries) to prevent people from leaving your company and to keep competitors away from them (by building an electrified perimeter fence). Third, protect the workforce. Use the employee assistance program to comfort folks and raise their morale against the expected storm (erect a tent and get everyone inside it). Fourth, call your stockholders. Reconstruct your broken cell phone so that it will allow you to make the call that will stop the takeover. You have 10 minutes to gather resources, 20 minutes before the initial attrition begins, 30 minutes before moral drops to an all time low, and 40 minutes until the takeover is complete. Any questions? Start whenever you are ready.

Action: Several subgroups gather resources, build perimeter fences, establish base camps by erecting tents, and call for help on toy cell phones.

Intent: Competition, cooperation, communication, time / resource management.

Note: This requires a very large indoor or outdoor space for large groups of 100.

Equipment: Assuming a group of 100 people in 4 subgroups, one shark suit (or similar animal attacker costume worn by a facilitator), 50 ethafoam noodles, 4 spools of lightweight wire, 4 self-standing tents (see #32), 4 pairs of toy phones, 4 screwdrivers, 4 wrenches, and 12 battery packs (8 for phones and 4 for wires).

Setup: One facilitator slips away to put on the shark suit and waits quietly out of sight until needed. The rest take the batteries out of the toy phones and carefully disassemble everything down to its component parts. All these parts are spread and hidden around the room. The group is gathered in the room and divided into subgroups according to their natural organizational structure (exactly equal sizes are not important). They then sit down in a close circle and select 10% of their subgroup membership to be their mobile leaders (3 leaders for a subgroup of 27). These leaders stand up and put on a blindfold. A copy of written instructions is given to each leader, who takes this back to the subgroup for them to read.

Task: To gather resources, build a fence, tent, and cell phone, then call for help.

Constraints: Leaders are blindfolded and may move freely. The rest are immobile and must remain in place.

Safety: Watch that blindfolded leaders don't trip over resources and hit or bump people with carried materials.

Facilitation: After reading the instructions, a mad dash to grab all the resources often follows. As a result, some subgroups do not get enough batteries to work their cell phones or to electrify their perimeter fences. After 20 minutes, the attrition shark periodically enters and attacks anyone not protected by a fence (they become observers). When the shark attacks blindfolded leaders or other influential individuals, the ensuing chaos encourages others to speed up their work and discourages some from thinking about sharing resources (just in case they need them later). All of this makes for a very interesting discussion about the myth of abundance and the more for me means less for you paradigm.

Variations: Instead of the tent, have them make a house of noodles, so these become less available for the electric fence.

99   **Debt Collection**

PROPS: 4   **TIME:** 120-240   **ALIAS:** Score Orienteering, NEW
MOVE: 3   **SIZE:** 10-100   **ORIGIN:** Bjorn Kellstrom

EQUIPMENT: The score orienteering map

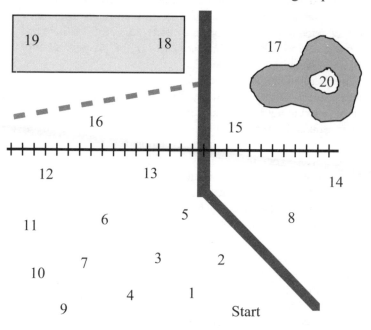

In this activity, your group goal is to collect $100,000 in outstanding debts in the next 60 minutes. On your master files (maps) is the location of twenty debtors (flags) and the amounts they owe (expressed in thousand dollar units), so that collecting all twenty debts could recover $210,000. To recover each debt, a pair of collectors will need to visit a debtor. Once there, they will be expected to demonstrate their sincerity and commitment to this process (by performing a small task and recording the result). Some of these debtors and debts may be more difficult to find and recover than others, but will these will inevitably return greater sums of money. You group will have 20 minutes to plan who will partner as paired collectors and which debtors they will visit. During this time, you will also need to copy the relevant locations into your files (copy from the master map as needed). You must return here after 60 minutes with your results and, if done correctly, to total the recoveries. For every minute that collectors are still out in the field, $1,000 will be lost from the final total. Any questions?

Action: Using a map and compass in the woods, pairs of people locate several flags worth different values.

Intent: Planning, problem solving, communication, cooperation, and partnering.

Note: A large outdoor area, like forested hilly land, and a high quality map of the area are necessary to conduct this activity. It can take up to half a day to complete. Orienteering uses a map and compass to calculate distances and directions to several marked flags and then actually visiting those flags in the field with the map and compass.

Equipment: One blank map (without flag locations drawn on it) and one compass for each person, one master map (with flags locations noted after flags are positioned) for each group, twenty small flags, and a marker. If tasks are to be performed and/or results recorded at each flag, a series of tasks and pen and paper will be needed.

Setup: Position the flags around the orienteering terrain and accurately record their location on the master maps. Assign values to the flags based on how difficult they will be to find and how distant they are from the start (1 = easy and close, while 20 = hard and far). If task performing and result recording are part of the activity, tasks will need to be placed with flags and their hardship calculated into the final values. Write these values on the flag on the map locations. Gather the groups, give them master maps, and a blank map and compass to each person.

Task: To send pairs to visit enough sites (values from $1,000 to $20,000) in order to total $100,000 per group in 60 minutes. Values can only be obtained if a task is performed at each site and the results are recorded correctly.

Constraints: For every minute you are late returning from your visits, your group will lose $1,000.

Safety: People will need to know (or be taught by the facilitator or others) how to read a map and use a compass.

Facilitation: Debrief for planning and execution of the plan. Discuss unexpected barriers and problems.

Variations: Tasks that can be used at the various flags include the typical parlor games of moving toothpicks, touching match boxes, balancing coins, changing numerals, or connecting dots. See also activities #4 through #15. Substitute for compasses by using G.P.S. units and Geocaching & Geoteaming are born!

100   Search & Rescue

PROPS: 4   **TIME:** 240-480   **ALIAS:** SAREx, NEW
MOVE: 4   **SIZE:** 10-100   **ORIGIN:** Simon Priest

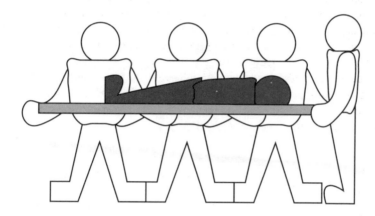

ACTION:
carrying a
stretcher

The leaders of your organization have failed to show up for a meeting and were last seen leaving for early morning runs by the resort security guard. An interview of this person has provided this information (distribute a description of the lost people). Since your leaders have failed to return, one must assume they're injured. Your task is to search the area designated on these maps (give a map to each group showing their areas of accountability and where the others will be searching), locate any lost people, treat their injuries and transport them back here to home base. Any questions so far?... Okay, if you locate injured people, someone in your group will need to take charge of the situation and the rest will need to perform three functions: trauma; temperature; and transport. Trauma will provide first aid, monitor vital signs, comfort and stabilize the victim. Temperature will boil water to warm any cold victims (who might be hypothermic from shock of the injury) or any exhausted searchers who get cold. Transport will build an appropriate stretcher and find an easy way to carry it out. So in summary, this exercise has two parts: search and rescue. In the search, you will navigate through your area of responsibility and look for lost people. In the rescue, you will treat injuries and return to here with any victims you should find. Your roles will change several times during the day. For example, everyone will be searching, even though only a minority of your group received this training, and everyone may be carrying a stretcher or boiling water to warm cold victims, even though the majority received no training at all in this skill. Any questions?

Action: Several groups locate their lost bosses, treat imaginary injuries with first aid, and evacuate them by stretchers.

Intent: Leadership, cross-training of skills, cooperation, communication, trust, risk taking, and adversity.

Note: A large outdoor area, like forested hilly land, and a map of the area are necessary to conduct this activity. The following information is provided as a reference guide and has been generalized to allow for a variety of scenarios. It can take a full day to complete with some time before the event used to cross-train people in four areas: navigation; search methods; first aid; and stretcher construction (see Setup on the next page). Each group of ten should have one trained to give first aid, two trained to construct stretchers, three trained to navigate, and four trained to conduct searches. Non-participants can supervise multiple groups from a central home base.

Equipment: People trained in navigation get a map and compass each. People trained in search methods share an accident response kit (bottle of water, aluminum pot, portable stove, tank of fuel, foam pad, sleeping bag, and emergency shelter). People trained in first aid share a first aid kit (manual, bandaids, butterfly closures, trauma dressings, scissors, gauze pads, gauze rolls, cloth tape, triangular bandages, elastic bandages, and wire splints). People trained in stretcher construction receive 50' of rope each. Each group gets packs to carry this equipment in. Radios or cell phones for each group and//or facilitator should prove helpful in commmunicating in the field.

Setup: Before the SAREx the four skill areas are taught to people and then these trained people have time to share their knowledge with one another. Facilitators act as further learning resources as needed. Although people have unique areas of expertise, they may all be searching or navigating at the start and some might have to assist with first aid and stretcher construction later on. So, cross training everyone in a group makes a great deal of sense.

1) FIRST AIDER = Teach and practice the ABCD's (airway, breathing, circulation, and diagnostic checklist) as well as all necessary paperwork (accident report, evacuation report, and vital sign monitoring forms).

2) STRETCHER CONSTRUCTORS = Teach and practice with a guinea pig three methods of making stretchers (poles and tarp, poles and rope, rope only) and how to find and flag an evacuation route.

3) NAVIGATORS = Teach and practice how to read the map (colors, symbols, field features, elevation contours, and distance scales) and how to use a compass (map bearings, field bearings, and declination adjustment).

4) SEARCH CONDUCTORS = Teach and practice two basic field procedures (hasty searches of high probability areas and coarse-line searches of an area in square grids). Give them the added responsibilities of conducting frequent head counts of their groups to avoid losing members.

After breakfast, the officers of the organization are quietly slipped away to a hidden location (see variations). A facilitator accompanies each one for the entire exercise. The facilitator has resources (book to read, sun or insect lotion, warm clothing, whistle, etc.) to keep them comfortable for what may be a long wait until searchers arrive.

Gather the group and remind them that this is a simulated exercise. In a real search and rescue situation, they would obtain professional assistance by contacting their local police. However, for the purpose of this activity only, they should assume that professional assistance is not an option. DO NOT DIAL 911! Should they meet any members of the public (not associated with this exercise), take a moment to inform them NOT to call the police! Also, encourage people to stay with their groups and never search alone. A lost searcher becomes a real situation.

Task: To navigate, search, and locate lost people and then to rescue (treat injuries and keep warm) or transport (evacuate by stretcher) any injured victims found, without losing or hurting any group or individual searchers.

Constraints: If searchers miss a lost person, or if time is running out, the lost person is instructed to blow a whistle three times (international distress signal) in order to bring the searchers closer. The lost person (now a victim) should feign injuries that would necessitate being carried by stretcher (like a broken leg or twisted ankle). Under normal circumstances, search groups should stay within their designated search areas as shown on their maps.

Safety: One facilitator remains with the non-searchers who coordinate operations from a home base. A facilitator accompanies each search group and together they should have a radio or cell phone for communication with home base.

Facilitation: Aside from all the teamwork within and among groups, discuss flexible cross training of skills versus fixed areas of responsibility. Debrief leadership changes between the search and rescue components of the activity and examine leadership without the boss (who was purposefully made the victim in this case).

Variations: This is much tougher to do inside. Popular outside hiding places have included: beneath piles of old leaves, under a fallen log, among large boulders, inside a small cave, and in the water under a footbridge (wearing a dry suit and PFD). Select locations based on local terrain and surrounding vegetation.

101   The Final Problem

PROPS: 3   **TIME:** 240-480   **ALIAS:** Wild Goose Chase, NEW
MOVE: 3   **SIZE:** 10-100   **ORIGIN:** Simon Priest

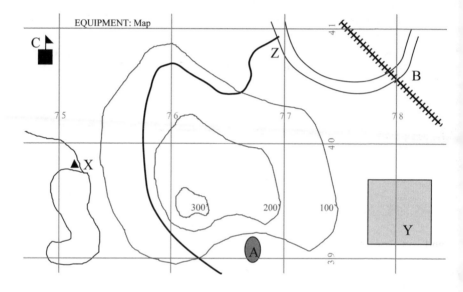

WRITTEN INSTRUCTIONS: *The following represent the 7 sites your group must visit. At each site, you will perform a task and gain valuable information that you can use toward finding the final problem to be solved.*

1. *A is in the center of the gravel pit by the rusty truck. (letters)*
2. *B is on the signal arm at the level railway crossing. (letters)*
3. *C is under the playground slide behind the school. (letters)*
4. *X is atop the rock on the far side of the lake outlet. (numbers)*
5. *Y is beside the lone tree in the middle of the field. (numbers)*
6. *Z is in front of the register at the hiking trailhead. (numbers)*

7. *The final problem is located at XYZ (grid reference and altitude). Use an anagram of ABC as the codeword.*

Action: Groups find special sites, perform tasks, obtain critical information and use this to solve a final problem.

Intent: Problem solving, cooperation, leadership, creativity, logical reasoning, and analytical thinking.

Note: A large outdoor area, like forested hilly land, and a map of the area are necessary to conduct this activity. Six groups can be sent to six different locations and then reassemble to compare notes, or all groups can visit all locations in a much longer more competitive scenario. This can take about half a day or longer to complete.

Equipment: FOR EACH GROUP: Map and clue sheet (as below), pen, paper, calculator (optional), radio or cell phone, and a handheld Global Positioning Satellite (GPS) unit with instructions (or a compass and knowledge of its use). Question sheets for each site, plus some supporting information in sealed envelopes (see variations).

Setup: Prepare the sites (see variations). Assemble the group and provide them with the map and written instructions opposite.

Task: To locate six sites (from the map and clue sheets), to obtain information from each site by visiting it, to use that information to determine a grid reference and codeword, to locate and visit that grid reference site, to provide that correct code word for authentication, and then to receive the final problem for solving with pen and paper.

Constraints: Information at each of the six sites is obtained by first completing an activity and/or mini-problem.

Safety: Each group should have a way to communicate with home base (radio, cell phone, or spare facilitator).

Facilitation: If a facilitator joins each group, then debriefing can be done on the run. If time is not a concern, hold occasional debriefs after each site has been visited. Discuss ongoing teamwork and leadership.

Variations: The tasks, activities and/or mini-problems at each location could be any of the activities in this book, pencil and paper exercises from many of the standard team building books, or the six questions (ABC and XYZ) listed below. Here are specific details for the codeword, grid reference, final problem, and final solution. As mentioned earlier, feel free to substitute your own tasks here.

Codeword

The Codeword is used to gain access to the final problem and will be authenticated by a person you meet there. It is created by anagramming the answers (or mixing up some of the letters) from A, B, and C.

A = A 6 letter word that does not use any of the 5 standard vowels (HINT: relates to music). Take all 5 consonants for use in the codeword. *ANSWER = rhythm, use RHYTM.*

B = A 9 letter word that uses all 5 standard vowels in alphabetical order (HINT: sarcasm). Take only the 3 unique consonants for use in the code word (do not take the repeat consonant). *ANSWER = facetious, use FCS.*

C = The 3 vowels that are next to one another on a standard keyboard (HINT: debt). *ANSWER = IOU*

Codeword = Unscramble the 8 consonants from A and B, along with the 3 vowels of C, to form either one 8 letter word or two 7 letter words. Give this codeword and/or these two backup words to the person who greets you once you locate the final problem site. If it is authenticated, you will gain access to the final problem. *SOME POSSIBLE ANSWERS = humorist (8), fourths, history, ostrich, tourism, mortify and thorium (7).*

Grid Reference

The Grid Reference is a six digit number that designates a precise map location where the final problem is to be found. It is obtained by combining X with Y, by using Z as the elevation, and by operating the GPS unit to find X, Y and Z.

X = Select 3 different digits between 1 and 9 (no zeros). Reverse this first number to get a second number. Subtract whichever of these two number is the lowest from the other highest one to obtain a third number. If the third number is only two digits, place a zero in front of it. Reverse this third number to get a fourth number. Add the third and fourth numbers together to get a fifth number. Open the envelope marked with an X and subtract the number inside (327) from the fifth number to get your answer. *ANSWER = 1089 - 327 = 762 or the first three digits of the grid reference (the task above is designed so that the fifth number will always be 1089 and facilitators can adjust the enveloped number accordingly).*

Y = Pick any 7 digit phone number of a person from your group. Scramble these seven digits in any order to create a random second phone number. Subtract the smaller phone number from the larger one to obtain a third number. Add the digits of this third number together to get a fourth number and then add the digits of the fourth number together to get a fifth number. Open the envelope marked Y and add the number inside (386) to your fifth number to get your answer. *ANSWER = 9 + 386 = 395 or the second three digits of the grid reference (the task above is designed so that the fifth number will always be 9 and facilitators can adjust the enveloped number accordingly).*

Z = Choose 3 different digits between 1 and 9 (like 000). Double these so they repeat to form a six digit second number (000000). Divide this second number by 13 to obtain a third number and divide this again by 7 to obtain a fourth number. Divide this fourth number by your original 3 digit first number to get a fifth number. Open envelope Z and multiply the number inside (30) by your fifth number to get your answer. *ANSWER = 11 X 30 = 330' or the altitude (the task above is designed so that the fifth number will always be 11 and facilitators can adjust the enveloped number accordingly).*

Therefore, the grid reference is 762395 (altitude of 330'). Enter these numbers into the GPS unit and continue to that location (*top of the hill*), where you submit your 8 letter codeword *(humorist)* or two of the 7 letter backup words. The Final Problem is a brain teaser that requires teamwork to complete and is explained along with a solution on the next pages.

The Final Problem

You are hiring for a new Director of Public Relations and unfortunately have confused pages from the application forms of five short listed managers. You know some basic information about each person such as their names, years in their present position, current department, assistant's name, preferred thinking style as identified by De Bono's 6 thinking hat colors, and the fact that they all have adjacent offices in the same hallway. With what you already know, who manages marketing, who has three years as a manager, and who follows intuition with a red thinking hat? *The information below appears in an order that makes the solution much easier. Randomize this sequence before presenting the clues to any group.*

1. The managers with the least and most years in their positions have offices at opposite ends of the line.
2. Zimmer has been a manager for nine years.
3. Leslie helps Zimmer.
4. Leslie is in an office beside a manager who facilitates with a blue hat.
5. Human resources is located in the middle office.
6. The Call Center manager has only been in that position for one year.
7. The one year manager has an office alongside the manager of seven years.
8. Quade has worked as a manager for eight years.
9. Vail is assisted by Al.
10. Peter's boss wears the white hat of facts and figures.
11. Information Technology is managed by Upton.
12. Kline wears the green hat of creativity.
13. Jane is an assistant in Finance and Accounting.
14. An optimistic manager with a yellow hat is in the office beside Debbie.

The Final Solution

The Final Solution is usually obtained by making a grid like the one below and using logic to eliminate options. *ANSWERS: Marketing = Zimmer, Three years = Upton, and Red hat = Vail:*

MANAGER	Zimmer	Upton	Quade	Kline	Vail
YEARS	Nine	Three	Eight	Seven	One
ASSISTANT	Leslie	Debbie	Peter	Jane	Al
HAT COLOR	Yellow	Blue	White	Green	Red
DEPARTMENT	Marketing & Sales	Information Technology	Human Resources	Finances & Accounting	Call Center

BONUS POINTS: Which letter of the alphabet did not appear anywhere in the final problem or solution (these two opposing pages)? *ANSWER = X.*

Other Publications from TARRAK Technologies

BOOKS for Experiential Learning

100 of the best Virtual Team-Building Events

99 of the best Experiential Corporate Games

Essential Elements of Facilitation

Electronic Facilitation

Global Leadership

INSTRUMENTS for Diagnosis & Research

Online Trust & Virtual Teamwork

Interpersonal Trust Assessment

Teamwork & Leadership

SOFTWARE for Working Online

Various Team Problems

Assorted Puzzles

Visit http://www.tarrak.com for a thorough updated list of products